HISTORY OF COMPUTING IN EDUCATION

IFIP – The International Federation for Information Processing

IFIP was founded in 1960 under the auspices of UNESCO, following the First World Computer Congress held in Paris the previous year. An umbrella organization for societies working in information processing, IFIP's aim is two-fold: to support information processing within its member countries and to encourage technology transfer to developing nations. As its mission statement clearly states,

> *IFIP's mission is to be the leading, truly international, apolitical organization which encourages and assists in the development, exploitation and application of information technology for the benefit of all people.*

IFIP is a non-profitmaking organization, run almost solely by 2500 volunteers. It operates through a number of technical committees, which organize events and publications. IFIP's events range from an international congress to local seminars, but the most important are:

- The IFIP World Computer Congress, held every second year;
- Open conferences;
- Working conferences.

The flagship event is the IFIP World Computer Congress, at which both invited and contributed papers are presented. Contributed papers are rigorously refereed and the rejection rate is high.

As with the Congress, participation in the open conferences is open to all and papers may be invited or submitted. Again, submitted papers are stringently refereed.

The working conferences are structured differently. They are usually run by a working group and attendance is small and by invitation only. Their purpose is to create an atmosphere conducive to innovation and development. Refereeing is less rigorous and papers are subjected to extensive group discussion.

Publications arising from IFIP events vary. The papers presented at the IFIP World Computer Congress and at open conferences are published as conference proceedings, while the results of the working conferences are often published as collections of selected and edited papers.

Any national society whose primary activity is in information may apply to become a full member of IFIP, although full membership is restricted to one society per country. Full members are entitled to vote at the annual General Assembly, National societies preferring a less committed involvement may apply for associate or corresponding membership. Associate members enjoy the same benefits as full members, but without voting rights. Corresponding members are not represented in IFIP bodies. Affiliated membership is open to non-national societies, and individual and honorary membership schemes are also offered.

HISTORY OF COMPUTING IN EDUCATION

IFIP 18th World Computer Congress
TC3 / TC9 1st Conference on the History of Computing in Education
22–27 August 2004
Toulouse, France

Edited by

John Impagliazzo
Hofstra University
USA

John A. N. Lee
Virginia Tech / Radford University
USA

SPRINGER SCIENCE+BUSINESS MEDIA, LLC

Library of Congress Cataloging-in-Publication Data

A C.I.P. Catalogue record for this book is available from the Library of Congress.

History of Computing in Education
Edited by John Impagliazzo and John A. N. Lee
ISBN 978-1-4419-5484-8 ISBN 978-1-4020-8136-1 (eBook)
DOI 10.1007/978-1-4020-8136-1

Printed on acid-free paper.

Dedication

This book is dedicated to

The men and women around the world who seek to preserve the legacy of their profession

and to

John A. N. Lee for his many years of dedicated service in the promotion of computing history throughout the global educational community and within IFIP.

Contents

Preface

This work derives from a conference discussing the history of computing in education. This conference is the first of hopefully a series of conferences that will take place within the International Federation for Information Processing (IFIP) and hence, we describe it as the First Conference on the History of Computing in Education (HCE1). These proceedings represent a collection of works presented at the HCE1 Conference held in association with the IFIP 2004 World Computer Congress held in Toulouse, France. Contributions to this volume range from a wide variety of educational perspectives and represent activities from four continents. The HCE1 conference represents a joint effort of the IFIP Working Group 9.7 on the History of Computing and the IFIP Technical Committee 3 on Education.

The HCE1 Conference brings to light a broad spectrum of issues and spans four continents. It illustrates topics in computing education as they occurred in the "early days" of computing whose ramifications or overtones remain with us today. Indeed, many of the early challenges remain part of our educational tapestry; most likely, many will evolve into future challenges. Therefore, this work provides additional value to the reader as it will reflect in part the future development of computing in education to stimulate new ideas and models in educational development.

The Program Committee of HCE1 received over thirty proposals to its call for participation. Subject to the constraints of the conference, it sought to provide a representation of the history or development of computing in education. The Program Committee believes that the eighteen papers appearing within these proceedings capture the essence of the historical panorama presented at the conference. It also considers this HCE1 event historic in itself as it attracted so many worthy proposals and published papers. Indeed, it looks forward to an exciting and enlightening discourse in Toulouse. The HCE1 program indicates that the efforts brought forward by all concerned will contribute to a very worthwhile event.

The HCE1 Program Committee expresses it gratitude to the organizers of the 2004 World Computer Congress for without their support, this conference would not be possible. The Committee looks forward to joining the presenters and attendees of the HCE1 conference and welcomes all participants to this historic event.

John Impagliazzo, New York, USA
John A. N. Lee, Virginia, USA

Program Committee Members

Peter Bollerslev, Denmark
Former IFIP President, (Chair, Program Committee)

John Impagliazzo, USA
Chair, IFIP WG 9.7

John A. N. Lee, USA
Founder, IFIP WG 9.7

Jan Wibe, Norway
Chair, IFIP TC3

Welcome

Welcome to HCE1 – the First Conference on the History of Computing in Education. HCE1 is one of several conferences held in association with the 2004 World Computer Congress of the International Federation for Information Processing (IFIP). We welcome you to this important event.

The title of this conference is fortuitously ambiguous. We may interpret it as either the "History of *Computing in Education*" or the "*History of Computing* in Education". The contributions reflect issues from authors from four continents and both these interpretations are well represented in the proceedings. Therefore, the papers allow us to look at the computing education from both points of view. At the same time, the diversity of viewpoints represented by the two sponsoring Technical Committees is apparent. The presentations allow individuals to learn about the history of computing in education in ways that will assist us in furthering the goals of the Technical Committee on Education (TC-3) and to examine the relationships between computers and society, which is the goal of Technical Committee 9.

This conference is a first for the IFIP World Computer Congress in the context of looking at the history of a topic of concern to a specific Technical Committee of IFIP. I hope that it will stand as a model for future meetings where we can look further at the history of computing and how that view can assist us both in furthering the work of IFIP committees and in charting a future course for study.

– *Peter Bollerslev*
HCE1 Program Chair

Acknowledgments

The editors appreciate the cooperation and diligence of the authors in the preparation of this volume; it was a pleasure to work with them and to learn more about the impact of the computer on education in the past years.

HISTORY OF COMPUTING IN EDUCATION

An Overview

John A.N. Lee
Virginia Tech and Radford University, USA
E-mail: janlee17@verizon.net

Abstract: This paper provides an overview of the history of computing and its affect on computing in education. It describes the evolution of the history of computing through activities such as conferences, collection and archival activities, individual collections, books and journals, and websites. It also illustrates the use of computers in the history of education in areas such as computing education, engineering, home and office, and the classroom. The paper brings light the importance of history in fulfilling the legacy of different areas of learning.

Key words: History of computing; Computing education; History; Education; Organizations; Museums; Virtual museums

1. INTRODUCTION

From the early general accessibility of the computer, there was a need for training in the methods of programming computers. The primary focus was on the retraining of mathematicians and engineers, as they were thought to have natural abilities to use calculators. Computers were simply extensions of the calculator medium. Interested parties of the time did not anticipate that computers would be much more than special calculators that had the ability to complete solutions to bigger problems in less time. Thus, computer education in the 1950s centered primarily on numerical methods and the ability to express solutions in the new language of computers. For many users, this was a fairly logical extension of the instructions that had been laid out for human computers to follow—those (generally female) workers who spent their days doing calculations to solve problems using tabular instruction sets prescribed by researchers or engineers. The use of computers in education developed initially as an extension of the general (commonly repetitive) problem solving exercises. For those of who were in college in the 1950s, they should recall that students became accustomed to the drudgery of solving daily problem exercise sets. The intent was to ensure that students understood the material they learned that day. Computer programming followed a different approach, akin to learning a topic by teaching it. If students could express the means for solving a problem by designing a program, then it meant that they also understood how to solve the problem themselves. To achieve this goal, it was also necessary to teach students the syntax of computer programming, whereas the ability to use of slide rules and calculators was assumed.

Perhaps as late as the mid-1960s, computers in education had not spread much wider than engineering, mathematics, and the emerging field of computer science. Then, the non-numeric use of computers started to grow and the availability of "personal computing" through time-sharing systems gave birth to the ideas of "computer aided instruction". While there were pockets of excellence in this field, CAI did not reach most locations until the advent of the world wide web.

The topic of this conference is the history of computing in education, with the expectation that we can review and document the impact of the computer on education. One portion of this documentation is the development of courses on the history of computing and the use of history as a tool in education.

2. HISTORY OF THE HISTORY OF COMPUTING

Many timelines and chronologies describe well the history of computing. Most sources are available through the world wide web. However, the history of the development of the field of the history of computing is less well known. One of the drawbacks has been the lack of recognition of the history of computing field as being appropriate at this stage of the development of the computer. Most historical studies view their field from a viewpoint of at least one hundred years, whereas computing is just about sixty years old and the most recent innovations that affect our daily lives are less than thirty years old. However, there were pioneers who decided that it was important to preserve the history of computing while both their colleagues and their artifacts were still around.

2.1 The Stages of Historical Preservation

History provides a reporting system that allows us to look back at our developments over the years and to use history to guide future progress. Computer history is lucky in one aspect that it is so recent that many of our pioneers still live and we have the opportunity to preserve their artifacts and documents. Computer history is unlucky in another aspect in that it is so recent that most professional historians disregard it and do not provide the impetus either to preserve our history or to apply their well-established techniques of analysis and scrutiny. Thus, the field of the history of computing has primarily been the domain of amateurs. Much of the preservation of computer history has been the hobby of enthusiasts who were not prepared to accept the tenet of the Virginia Department of Historic Resources that nothing after 1865, the date of the end of the American Civil War, is history!

2.1.1 Conferences

The 1973 Los Alamos Conference on the *History of Computing in the Twentieth Century* organized by Nick Metropolis was perhaps the earliest significant step in the preservation of the history of computing. The meeting brought together a large number of computer pioneers. Richard Hamming best expressed the theme of the meeting in his keynote presentation where he suggested that the reason for the gathering was "that we would know what they thought when they did it" [Metropolis et al, 1980]. While the proceedings were not available until seven years after the conference, the impetus it provided was momentous.

The first conference on the *History of Programming Languages*, organized in 1978 by Jean Sammet and J.A.N. Lee, was a direct consequence of the Los Alamos conference and the first organized by a professional society [Wexelblat, 1981]. It was the first of what most hoped to be a series of meetings in the style "The History of ..." organized by the Association for Computing Machinery, bringing together pioneers from specific fields. This 1978 meeting was important for bringing out a number of significant revelations, not the least of which was the announcement by Capt. Grace Murray Hopper of the preservation of the first computer bug. Later conferences included the histories of included the *History of Medical Informatics*, and the *History of Personal Workstations*, as well as a second *History of Programming Languages* conference in 1993 [Bergin, et al, 1996].

In 1976, the American Federation of Information Processing Societies (AFIPS) initiated Pioneer Days at the behest of Jean Sammet, the chair of the AFIPS History of Computing Committee (HOCC). In association with the National Computer Conferences they included the following areas[Sammet, 1985]:

1974 Dartmouth Time-sharing System
1975 Institute for Advanced Study and the IAS Computer
1976 ENIAC
1977 Los Alamos Scientific Laboratory
1978 Standards Western Automatic Computer (SWAC)
1979 COBOL
1980 The Founding of SHARE
1981 UNIVAC
1982 The Stored Program Concept and the 25th Anniversary of FORTRAN
1983 Howard Aiken and the Harvard Computation Laboratory
1984 Lawrence Livermore National Laboratory
1985 The First Illinois Computers

On 31 December 1990, AFIPS dissolved, and while constituent societies had taken over some of the other elements of the organization, Pioneer Days were not. Upon the founding of IFIP Working Group 9.7 in 1992, Pioneer Days was to become an integral part of IFIP World Computer Congresses. The concept received the enthusiastic support of Gesellschaft fur Informatik (GI) in Hamburg in 1994, led by Klaus Brunnstein. Intended for the host country to recognize and publicize their contributions to the history of computing, WCC Pioneer Days have taken place in 1994 (Germany), 1996 (Australia), 1998 (Austria/Hungary), and 2000 (China).

Perhaps the longest continuum of national history conferences was the French *Colloque sur l'Histoire de l'Informatique* soon to have its seventh meeting (ESAT, Cesson-Rennes, 16-18 November 2004). These meetings were primarily the child of Pierre Mounier-Kuhn (CNAM). More recently, John Impagliazzo, current chair of IFIP Working Group 9.7, has organized meetings and a conference on the *History of Nordic Computing* in 2003 June. He is encouraging other conferences in Europe and elsewhere.

2.1.2 Collection and Archival Activities

The Museum of History and Technology (now the National Museum of American History) of the Smithsonian Institute had been accepting bits and pieces of computer history when in 1970 AFIPS approached them with a proposition, written by Walter Carlson to initiate an oral history project. Hank Tropp of Humboldt State University became the curator for this project and conducted over 250 oral interviews by the time they dissolved the project in 1973. Unfortunately, many these interviews are still not publicly available. However, the Smithsonian moved forward with a project to develop a public exhibit that opened in 1990 called the "Information Age". This exhibit wisely contains dual tracks of communications and computers that eventual merge in the display. With constant updates, this exhibit is still very popular.

In the late 1970s Gwen and Gordon Bell convinced the Digital Equipment Corporation to establish a small display of devices in the foyer of the plant in Marlborough, Massachusetts. Their displays soon exceeded the available space. Hence, with DEC funding, they moved to establish the Computer Museum in Boston where it had many successful years. Whilst their collections and displays were magnificent, one of the greatest initiatives was the annual "Computer Bowl" that was not only a great fund raising venture, but also a fantastic learning opportunity shared by many college students. In 1996 the collections were moved to the West Coast and now became the initial elements of the Computer History Museum in Mountain View, California. Established in 1996, the Computing History Museum is a public benefit organization dedicated to the preservation and celebration of computing history. It is home to one of the largest collections of computing artifacts in the world, a collection comprising over 4,000 artifacts, 10,000 images, 4,000 linear feet of cataloged documentation and gigabytes of software [CHM www].

The Science Museum, London, includes a Computing and Information Technology collection that is perhaps most famous (today) for the reconstruction of the Babbage Difference Engine No. 2. Computing and Information Technology covers the devices, machines and systems from 1623 (first mechanical calculator) to the present. Its scope includes electromechanical and electronic calculation, analog and digital computation, data management and processing, and cryptography [SML www].

Also in the UK, the Computer Museum at Bletchley Park claims to be the UK's only hands-on exhibition of computing hardware and software technology. It traces the development of the computer from its origins with the Colossus, invented during the Second World War to break Lorenz codes through the mainframes of the 1960s, mini computers, homebuilt micros to the PC's of today. The vast majority of our exhibits are operational [CMB www].

The Heinz Nixdorf Museums Forum in Paderborn, Germany HNF, claims to be the largest computer museum in the world, and is also an important conference center. The exhibition rooms begin on the first floor charting the development of the cultural technologies of calculating, writing, and drawing up through the invention of the first computer. The second floor builds on the first-floor displays through the representation of the development, dissemination, and application of electronic data processing. The last fifty years of the development of information and communications technology unfold in this room and convey a sense of the ever-increasing pace of technological innovation [HNM www].

A number of companies have established their own museums, primarily to display their own products or use of their products. The Intel Museum is located in Santa Clara, California, and features a new exhibit highlighting 35 years of Intel corporate history and innovation. Several smaller semi-public computer museums also exist (or used to exist) in California, particularly the ones established by Apple Computer, Hewlett-Packard Corporation, IBM, Intel Corporation, and the Lawrence Livermore National Laboratories. Some museums are still in operation, some are in suspended animation, and some are just plain gone—meaning, paradoxically, that computers, or other artifacts from their own collections, may be in danger. While many museums have worked hard at fulfilling their stated purposes, none of them has ever aspired to the global treatment of California's computing [CHAC www].

Several university-based collections including the University of Amsterdam, the American University (Washington DC), and others also exist. For example, Professor Gabriel Robins conceived and created the University of Virginia's Computer Museum; Robins also serves as its curator. The museum contains various computer-related artifacts, both historical and modern. Most of the artifacts shown there are physically located in display cases in the hallways of the Department of Computer Science (Olsson Hall) at the University of Virginia.

As another example, a coalition of Stanford computer scientists has installed exhibits within the Gates Computer Science building containing historical equipment and documents focusing on Stanford's role in the history of computing. The exhibits change and become updated as time permits. The first exhibit, installed November 1997, focuses on the early history of the Stanford Computer Science Department, its founder George Forsythe, and his students [Stanford www].

The Charles Babbage Institute is an historical archives and research center of the University of Minnesota. CBI is dedicated to promoting study of the history of information technology and information processing and their impact on society. CBI preserves relevant historical documentation in all media, conducts and fosters research in history and archival methods, offers graduate fellowships, and sponsors symposia, conferences, and publications. The archival collection consists of corporate records, manuscript materials, records of professional associations, oral history interviews, trade publications, periodicals, obsolete manuals and product literature, photographs, films, videos, and reference materials. CBI also serves as a clearinghouse for resources on the history of information technology [CBI www].

2.1.3 Private Collections

The American Computer Museum, Bozeman, Montana, opened in 1990 as a U.S. non-profit corporation. Originally, the developers planned the museum to be in Princeton, New Jersey, but after looking at the tourism in the area the founders moved it to Bozeman. Located in beautiful Montana, the museum draws thousands of visitors from all fifty states and over fifty countries. With Yellowstone National Park to the south and Glacier National Park to the northwest, the museum is part of sightseeing itineraries by visitors worldwide. From its inception, the American Computer Museum has emphasized the evolution of the information age with an emphasis on the United States. Nevertheless, there are ample displays throughout the museum that highlight the contributions made by other nations and cultures to the rise of the information age. The American Computer Museum has been written about in many publications including, *The New York Times, The New Yorker Magazine, The Los Angeles Times, PC Week, QST Magazine,* and *USA Today* (ACMB www).

The DigiBarn Computer Museum seeks to capture personal stories and track technological evolution through a large collection of vintage computer systems, manuals, videos, interviews, and other fossil relics of the "Cambrian explosion" of personal computing that ignited in 1975. The organizers claim that "When we get visitors who 'burst into tears' upon seeing certain systems which may have defined their lives and careers, our cameras roll to capture the inevitable stories. Thus, the interconnected redwood rooms of the museum constitute a kind of "memory palace" for the nerd-inclined and help us piece together the amazing story of the invention of personal computing and Cyberspace." [DBCM www] The DigiBarn is a ninety plus years old barn constructed of old growth redwood that is part of the original "Ancient Oaks Ranch", a 19th century farmstead nestled deep in the Santa Cruz Mountains of Northern California.

2.1.4 Books and Journals

Like computing itself, the history of computing has taken a set of brave publishers to have the faith in sales and marketing to justify the printing of books appropriate to school and college courses. Regrettably, publishers do not often reprint these books and many excellent texts are no longer available. However, the collection is growing steadily, though the interest in more recent history far outweighs the longer views. The field has the support of only one journal, the IEEE *Annals of the History of Computing*, published since 1978; it is a superior source of materials. Recently the IEEE Computer Society has digitized the issues back to 1978 and made them available through their digital library. Occasionally, articles appear in other professional journals, but frequently they have not had the review and editing that is necessary to check the validity of the information.

The same is true of textbooks targeted to the beginning computing courses, and many myths of computing continue to promulgate through the lack of qualified reviewers. The references to this paper document many of the available books and other resources.

2.1.5 Web Sites

American University Computing History Museum and its website originated in 1999 to support the historiography of programming languages and software engineering [AUCHM www]. Supported by a multi-year grant from the Alfred E. Sloan Foundation, the original site was part of the HotNet Project, which provided funding to universities to create web sites to support the historiography of various technologies.

The Virtual Museum of Computing [VMC www] includes an eclectic collection of world wide web hyperlinks connected with the history of computing and online computer-based exhibits available both locally and around the world. This museum opened on 1 June 1995 and has expanded to cover many non-computer specific museums. The site includes an extremely useful set of links to many other museums.

Smaller virtual museums include many university collections such as the Computer Museum at the University of Queensland [CMQ www], which primarily contains a collection of documents and images tracing the development of computers and their associated peripherals from the early 1960s, when they installed a General Electric Model GE225 as the first digital computer at the University and in Queensland. As a source of certain "old" documents, this may be very useful to students

3. COMPUTERS IN THE HISTORY OF EDUCATION

3.1.1 Computing Education

Howard Aiken at Harvard University was probably the first to offer computer courses. His courses centered primarily on numerical applications with programming and the computer was more of a calculation tool along with the calculator and slide rule. In the early 1960s, computer science programs began to appear in US universities, though frequently the field appeared as a sub-discipline of mathematics or engineering in many institutions. As a service discipline, they commonly taught programming to those who had applications, and research in computing was concentrated on hardware and numeric applications. It was not until the late 1960s that they followed pursuits that were more theoretical and even later they began to view software engineering as vogue.

3.1.2 Computers in Engineering

Engineers have always had the difficulty of finding the means to do computation based on problem solving for the analysis and design of their products. Thus, engineers were among the first to recognize the usefulness of computers and, typical of their approach to other needs, frequently chose to be the teachers of their own students. Even as ardent users of computer engineers were not forward in using computers in education.

3.1.3 Computers in the Office

In the office, computers were slow in acceptance, though the advent of time-sharing and the emergence of text editing systems such as IBM SCRIPT accelerated the infusion in the late 1970s. Like many other fields, the introduction of the personal computer provided a large impetus to have computers replace typewriters and consequently, it raised the need for training for office staff. Distinct from general education, training for office staff did not include instruction in the fundamentals and concepts of the field. Thus, much of office training dealt with computer-based systems. The success of these systems has led to their being available to students in schools and colleges so that they could attain skill levels that depend more on demonstration and exercise than on understanding and comprehension.

3.1.4 Computers in the Classroom

Computer Aided Instruction (CAI) has been a long time goal of the computer area, originating probably in the early 1960s. However, it did not really become practical until the introduction of the world wide web. In the early days perhaps the most effective CAI systems were the business games that simulated various industries, the most common being the "widget" business that allowed students to simulate their involvement in various aspects of a manufacturing and marketing company. Commonly used in summer schools for students in business schools or for executives in MBA-style programs, one could play them over long periods and integrate the games into the general curriculum. These still exist in the form of the "SIM" products and in other invocations.

The PLATO system, started back in 1960, became a technological solution to deliver individualized instruction in thousands of subjects from algebra to zoology to students in schools and universities across the nation. As the system grew and evolved, it became, pretty much by accident, the first major online community, in the current sense of the term. In the early 1970s, people lucky enough to have exposure to the system discovered that it offered a radically new way of understanding the use of computers; computers were not just about number-crunching (and delivering individualized instruction). They were about people connecting with people. For many PLATO people who came across PLATO in the 1970s, this was a mind-blowing concept.

The PLATO system finds its origins in the early 1960s at the University of Illinois at Urbana. Don Bitzer, its developer, was an electrical engineering professor who had an interest in using computers for teaching. Together with several colleagues, they founded the Computer-based Education Research Laboratory (CERL). The original PLATO system was comprised of custom developed hardware and software and was one of the first time-sharing systems. In 1972, they ported the software to a more powerful mainframe platform with support for hundreds of simultaneous users. As the Control Data Corporation ran into financial trouble in the late 1980s and microcomputers became a more cost-effective platform than mainframes, many PLATO systems closed down. The PLATO name was sold to a Minneapolis-based company called PLATO Learning, Inc. Control Data's PLATO system was renamed CYBIS, and continued to be supported at several university and government sites still running the original PLATO Notes software. The University of Illinois PLATO system was renamed NovaNET, and transferred to a private company called NovaNET Learning, Inc., of Tucson, Arizona [Nova www].

With the advent of the world wide web, new teaching/testing systems developed that provided a myriad of customized services that supported a computer aided teaching/learning environment. For example, Blackboard offers a complete suite of enterprise software products and services that power e-education programs in primary markets such as pre-college, college, university, corporate/government, and international education programs. Blackboard solutions deliver the promise of the internet for online teaching and learning, campus communities, campus commerce services, and integration of web-enabled student services and back office systems [Blackboard www].

WebCT claims to be the leading provider of e-learning solutions for higher education. It began as an educator's dream to provide students with a flexible, integrated environment where teachers could use the latest technology to foster inquiry, encourage discourse, and inspire collaboration. Today, its mission is to help institutions deliver on their commitment to educational excellence with enterprise-wide learning management solutions that integrate the richest and most flexible pedagogical tools with existing campus infrastructure [WebCT www].

Students studying calculus, linear algebra, and other mathematics subjects at Virginia Tech have been engaged in exciting new ways to learn through the Math Emporium [MathEmp www]. Established in 1997 in a disused department store site, the Emporium contains 500 machines arranged in pods of five systems. Each pod is dedicated to a specific course topic and allows students to share experiences as they undertake their learning and practice. The emporium developed on faculty members' years of experience as teachers. It also used their years of increasing experience with computer technology and course innovations for which the mathematics department and individual faculty members have won numerous awards. From the outset, students know the learning goals of a course plus important learning milestones they must meet. They set their own schedules. They learn at their own pace. They receive immediate feedback on quizzes and problems. They explore alternative approaches to learning challenging material. They interact one-on-one with faculty and other students. They master coursework as well as -- and often better -- than in conventional classrooms.

The Math Emporium is a facility with 500 high-performance dual-platform computers arranged in state-of-the-art workstations. Customized, easy-to-use computer programs guide students through their coursework, allowing them to breeze through material they quickly master and to concentrate their time on more challenging concepts. In addition, students can work individually or in groups of up to eight students, giving all students the opportunity to create the best match between their learning environment and their own learning style. Students also have the opportunity to work one-on-one with professors and with graduate and undergraduate student coaches as much or as little as they need. Studies have shown that students using technology in mathematics courses typically outperform their peers in traditional classroom settings. However, because it is new and experimental, professors are studying and assessing Math Emporium activities closely to find out what works well and what elements of it they can improve. Faculty members individually monitor students' progress through their course work to ensure that no one falls behind. Students' comments and concerns receive top priority in creating or refining coursework and computer software.

Another form of CAI tool is the simulators that are commonly used in military systems or flight training. While most such simulators primarily intend to provide a hands-on experience, there is a growing trend to the use of simulators in the classroom to understand better concepts and fundamentals of complex systems. As the complexity and variety of computer system hardware increases, its suitability as a pedagogical tool in computer organization/architecture courses diminishes. Consequently, many instructors are turning to simulators as teaching aids. They often use valuable teaching/research time to construct them. Many of these simulators are freely available on the Internet, providing a useful and timesaving resource for other instructors. However, finding the right simulator for a particular course or topic can itself be a time-consuming process [Wolffe, 2002]. Beyond computer science, simulators are useful in role-playing environments, gaming, and business simulations [Krauss, 1999]. Using SimCity and Sim2000 from Electronic Arts, students learn to build simulated cities and get hands-on experience meeting the challenges presented in city administration such as zoning, taxing, budgeting, power, transportation, pollution, crime, and land value.

3.1.5 Computers in the Home

As in the office, computers came into the home with the advent of the personal computer. Driven primarily by young people, the computer in the home has become almost as pervasive as the telephone and the television. An August 2003 survey by the Pew Internet Project [Pew, 2003] reported on the following results.

- 63% of Americans now go online. That amounts to 47% growth in the U.S. adult population using the internet, from 86 million in March 2000 to 126 million in August 2003.
- 52% of internet users go online on a typical day, as of August 2003. That figure amounts to 66 million people and has grown from 52 million who were online during a typical day in March 2000.
- 87% of U.S. internet users said they have access at home, and 48% said they have access at work.
- 25% said they use the internet at times from some place other than home or work in a March–May 2003 survey.
- 31% of internet users who go online from home have broadband access.

With numerous school systems in the U.S. now providing computers to their students, the extension of the school into the home for out-of-school assignments has extended the use of computers in education in the home.

4. SUMMARY

The history of computing in educations has many facets. From the early days, people viewed computers as sophisticated number crunchers and as extensions of calculators. Hence, computer education in the 1950s consisted of numerical methods for solving mathematical and scientific problems. After the mid-1960s, non-numeric use of computers started to grow. Once "personal computing" became available and time-sharing systems became pervasive, new ideas began to emerge. This gave birth to "computer aided instruction", perhaps the historical hallmark of the dynamic use of computers in an educational environment.

It should be clear that from historical beginnings to the uses of computing today, teachers at all levels should be mindful of the emergence of computing in the courses they teach, its place in the curriculum, and its function in the full educational program of their students. One way of doing this is to include vignettes of computing history in the courses they teach. For example, in a music class, could have students the history of the use of computers in the music composition. The discovery of the Moog Synthesizer may fascinate budding students and perhaps encourage them to seek further ways in which they could use computers in music development. The same is true for other areas of learning. Computing history can add new dimensions to existing courses by connecting modern technology to the subject at hand.

Professional organizations should also be mindful of roots of computing in their respective areas. For example, it would be useful to see know how computers first affected the areas such as accounting, architecture, and medicine. Unfortunately, the historical aspects professional activity is not a priority and often ignored. Even in computing, one would think that the preservation of its own beginnings and evolution should meaningful. Alas, only few organizations address this dimension of the computing field. Fortunately, some do. For example, the IEEE Computer Society, while not primarily a history organization, has been a leading light in the recognition of computer pioneers by initiating the Computer Pioneer Award in 1980. The recipients have included many well-known persons as well as some who were much more in the background but truly worthy of recognition. While other computing organizations worldwide have recognized pioneers in their field, such recognition has not become a priority in the work that they do. Perhaps in time, other societies will recognize the need for being historically proactive and present a stimulus for its members and associates.

In summary, the history of computing is important to learning in all fields of education, especially in computing education. The hope is that this message will stimulate interest in young and veteran scholars and provide a legacy for future generations.

ACKNOWLEDGEMENTS

The author is grateful for the invitation of conference to present this invited paper, and of the encouragement and support of John Impaglizzo, Peter Bollerslev, and Jan Wibe to create this overview as both my "swan song" and my version of Captain Hook's last speech!

REFERENCES

ACMB, 2004, American Computer Museum, Bozeman, Montana. http://www.compustory.com/american_computer_museum.htm, undated, last accessed 14 April 2004.
AUCHM, 2004, American University Computing History Museum. http://www.computinghistory museum.org/, undated, last accessed 14 April 2004.
Aspray, William, 1990, *Computing Before Computers*. Iowa State University Press, 1990.
Babbage, Charles. 1961, *On the Principles and Development of the Calculator and Other Seminal Writings* by Charles Babbage and Others. Dover Publications, 1961.
Bashe, Charles J., Lyle R. Johnson, John H. Palmer, and Emerson W. Pugh, 1968, *IBM's Early Computers*. Cambridge, Mass.: MIT Press
Baum, Claude, 1981, *The System Builders: The Story of SDC*. Santa Monica, CA: System Development Corporation.
Bergin, Thomas J., Gibson, Richard (eds), 1996, *History Of Programming Languages*. Reading, Mass.: Addison-Wesley.
Blackboard, undated, http://www.blackboard.com/about/index.htm
Campbell-Kelly, Martin and William Aspray, 1996, *Computer: A History of the Information Machine*. New York, NY:Basic Books.
Campbell-Kelly, Martin, Mary Croarken, Raymond Flood, Eleanor Robson, 2003, *The History of Mathematical Tables: From Sumer to Spreadsheets*. Oxford, UK: Oxford University Press.
Campbell-Kelly, Martin, 2003, *From Airline Reservations to Sonic the Hedgehog: A History of the Software Industry*. Cambridge, MA.:MIT Press.
CBI, Charles Babbage Institute, 2004, http://www.cbi.umn.edu/about/mission.html, undated, last accessed 14 April 2004.
Ceruzzi, Paul E., 1998, *A History of Modern Computing*. Cambridge, MA: The MIT Press.
Ceruzzi, Paul, E., 1983, *Reckoners: The Prehistory of the Digital Computer, from Relays to the Stored Program Concept, 1935-1945*. Westport,CT: Greenwood Press.
Chapuis, Robert J. and Amos E. Joel, Jr., 1990, *Electronics, Computers and Telephone Switching, Part III*. Amsterdam, New York, Oxford: North-Holland Publishing Company.
CMQ, 2004, Computer Museum at the University of Queensland. http://www.computer.museum .uq.edu.au/, undated, last accessed 14 April 2004.
Cohen, I. Bernard, and Gregory W. Welch, 1999, *Makin' Numbers: Howard Aiken and the Computer*. Cambridge, MA: The MIT Press.

Cohen, I. Bernard, 1999, *Howard Aiken: Portrait of a Computer Pioneer*. Cambridge, MA: The MIT Press.

CHAC, 2004, Computer History Association of California. http://www.chac.org/chintro.html, undated, last accessed 14 April 2004.

CHM, 2004, Computer History Museum. http://www.computerhistory.org/about/index.page, undated, last accessed 14 April 2004.

CMB, 2004, Computer Museum at Bletchley Park. http://www.retrobeep.com/, undated, last accessed 14 April 2004.

DeLamarter, Richard Thomas, 1986, *Big Blue: IBM's Use and Abuse of Power*, New York: Dodd, Mead.

DBCM, 2004, DigiBarn Computer Museum. http://www.digibarn.com/about.html, undated, last accessed 14 April 2004.

Englebourg, Saul, 1976, *International Business Machines: A Business History*. New York: Arno Press. Orig. pub. as a Ph.D. thesis, Columbia University, 1954.

Fisher, Franklin, M., James W. McKie, and Richard B. Mancke, 1983, *IBM and the U. S. Data Processing Industry: An Economic History*. New York: Praeger.

Fishman, Katherine Davis, 1981, *The Computer Establishment*. New York: Harper & Row.

Forman, Richard L., 1985, *Fulfilling the Computer's Promise: The History of Informatics, 1962-1968*. Woodland Hills, California.: Informatics

Freiberger, Paul and Michael Swaine, 2000, *Fire in the Valley: The Making of the Personal Computer*, second edition. New York, NY: McGraw-Hill.

Hall, Eldon C., 1996, *Journey to the Moon: The History of the Apollo Guidance Computer*. American Institute of Aeronautics and Astronautics.

HNM, undated, Heinz Nixdorf Museums Forum. http://hnf.paderborn.museum/

Hodges, Andrew, 1983, *Alan Turing: The Enigma*. New York, NY: Simon & Schuster.

Ifrah, George, 1999, *The Universal History of Numbers: From Prehistory to the Invention of the Computer*. New York: John Wiley & Sons.

Ifrah, George, 2001, *The Universal History of Computing: From the Abacus to the Quantum Computer*. New York, NY: John Wiley & Sons.

Imlay, John P., Jr. with Dennis Hamilton, 1994, *Jungle Rules: How to be a Tiger in Business*. New York, NY: Dutton.

Kestin, Hesh, 1992, *21st Century Management: The Revolutionary Strategies that Have Made Computer Associates a Multi-Billion Dollar Software Giant*. New York, NY: The Atlantic Monthly Press.

Krauss, Michael, 1999, *Simulating Real World Environments*. http://www.lclark.edu/~krauss /tesol98/sim.html

Kurtzig, Sandra L. with Tom Parker, 1991, *CEO: Building a $400 Million Dollar Company from the Ground Up*. New York, NY: W. W. Norton & Company.

Lammers, Susan, 1986, *Programmers at Work: Interviews with 19 Programmers Who Shaped the Computer Industry*. Washington, D.C.: Tempus, Redmond.

Lee, John A.N, 1995, *Computer Pioneers*. Los Alamitos CA: IEEE Computer Society Press.

Levering, Robert, Michael Katz, and Milton Moskowitz, 1984, *The Computer Entrepreneurs*. New York: New American Library.

Levy, Steven, 1984, *Hackers: Heroes of the Computer Revolution*. Norwell, MA: Anchor Press.

Manes, Stephen and Paul Andrews, 1993, *Gates: How Microsoft's Mogul Reinvented an Industry — and Made Himself the Richest Man in America*. New York, NY: Doubleday.

MathEmp, Math Emporium, 2004, http://www.emporium.vt.edu/emporium/newVisitor/index.html, undated, last accessed 14 April 2004.
Maurice V. Wilkes, 1995, *Memoirs of a Computer Pioneer*. Cambridge, MA: MIT Press.
McCartney, Scott, 1999, *ENIAC: The Triumphs and Tragedies of the World's First Computer*. New York, NY: Walker Publishing.
Metropolis, Nicholas, J. Howlett, and Gian-Carlo Rota, eds., 1980, *A History of Computing in the Twentieth Century*, New York: Academic Press.
Nova, 2004, NovaNET Learning. http://livinginternet.com/r/ri_talk.htm, undated, last accessed 14 April 2004.
Nyce, James M. and Paul Kahn, 1991, *From Memex to Hypertext: Vannevar Bush and the Mind's Machine*. New York, NY: Academic Press.
Pew Internet Project, December 22, 2003, America's Online Pursuits: The changing picture of who's online and what they do. http://www.pewinternet.org/reports/toc.asp?Report=106
Phister Jr., Montgomery. 1979. *Data Processing: Technology and Economics*. Santa Monica, Calif.: Digital Press and Santa Monica Publishing Co.
Pugh, Emerson W., 1995, *Building IBM: Shaping an Industry and Its Technology*. Cambridge, MA: MIT Press.
Riordan, Michael and Lillian Hoddeson, 1997, *Crystal Fire: The Birth of the Information Age*. New York, NY: W.W. Norton & Company.
Rojas, Rual, Ulf Hashagen (eds), 2002, *The First Computers—History and Architectures*. Cambridge, MA: MIT Press.
Sammet, Jean E., 1969, *Programming Languages: History and Fundamentals*. Englewood Cliffs, N.J.: Prentice-Hall.
Sammet, Jean E., 1985, Answers to Self-Study Questions. *Annals of the History of Computing*, Vol. 7, No. 4, p. 361.
SML, 2004, Science Museum London. http://www.sciencemuseum.org.uk/collections /subject_themes/computing.asp, undated, last accessed 14 April 2004.
Sobel, Robert, 1981, *IBM: Colossus in Transition*. New York: Times Books.
Stanford, undated, Stanford University, Gates Computer Science Building. http://www-db.stanford.edu /pub/voy/museum.html
U. S. Department of Commerce, 1984, *A Competitive Assessment of the United States Software Industry*. Washington, D.C.: U.S. Department of Commerce.
VMC, 2004, Virtual Museum of Computing. http://vmoc.museophile.org, undated, last accessed 14 April 2004.
WebCT, 2004, http://www.webct.com /company, undated, last accessed 14 April 2004.
Wexelblat, R. L., 1981, *History of Programming Languages*. New York, London: Academic Press.
Williams, M.R., 1997, *A History of Computing Technology*, Second Edition. Los Alamitos CA: IEEE Computer Society Press.
Wolffe, Gregory S., William Yurcik, Hugh Osborne, and Mark A. Holliday, 2002, Teaching computer organization/architecture with limited resources using simulators. *Proceedings of the 33rd SIGCSE Technical Symposium on Computer Science Education*, Cincinnati, Kentucky, pp. 176-180

THE CONTEST OF FACULTIES

Cybernetics vs. Informatik in German Universities

Wolfgang Coy
Humboldt-Universität zu Berlin, Germany
E-mail: coy@hu-berlin.de

Abstract: The discipline of cybernetics spans a field where information theory, general systems theory, or digital computers could be integrated. In a series of important conferences Norbert Wiener's approach toggled between the idea of a new universal science describing everything from radio receivers to psychology or ethnography and a formal mathematical model for well-defined information processes and control. In consequence cybernetics did not achieve the status of a faculty of its own.

The growing use of data processing equipment demonstrated a need for computer specialists on all levels of education. US-Universities reacted with the introduction of computer science, computer engineering, or information science courses and curricula. Germany followed US-curricula, but copied the name *Informatik* from the 1967 French Academy's definition of *informatique*. The new discipline started successfully 1969 in Germany with federal funding for eighteen university working groups, accelerating the decline of cybernetics.

Key words: Computer Science Curricula; Cybernetics; Informatics

1. INTRODUCTION

1.1 A New Field of Research: Electronic Brains

Alan Turing's epochal paper culminated in universal machines, a notion sometimes over-interpreted. John von Neumann transformed this logical construct into a set of practical guidelines. The von Neumann-architecture still serves as framework for actual computers though von Neumann investigated other concepts like cellular automata and self-reproducing machinery.

Norbert Wiener also thought about digital machinery and universal concepts, but Vannevar Bush, MIT-colleague and presidential advisor, declined Wiener's wartime proposal recognizing its engineering dimensions and directed him to the more promising concept of self-controlling anti-aircraft guns. Basic element of these machines was a "feed-back circuit," a notion not completely new (see fig. 1), but in its simple elegance applicable in many fields beyond anti-aircraft guns.

Figure 1. The Ouroboros, the "tail-devourer", an alchemistic symbol of the feed-back mechanism; here in a 15th century manuscript in Greek language.

Parallel to his wartime technological work, Wiener developed a theoretical approach that he published in 1948 in his text *Cybernetics, or Control and Communication in the Animal and the Machine.* His fresh approach, integrating information theory, general systems theory, and digital computers, was introduced into to a series of Macy-conferences with a number of investigators from very different fields. Wiener's concepts were not very focused at that time. They toggled between the idea of a new universal science describing everything from radio receivers to psychology and ethnography (represented e.g. by Gregory Bateson or Margaret Mead) and a strictly formal mathematical model for well-defined information processes and control. Wiener was not the only protagonist of these new concepts. Bateson (1967) notes: "The ideas were generated in many places: in Vienna by Bertalanffy, in Harvard by Wiener, in Princeton by von

Neumann, in Bell Telephone labs by Shannon, in Cambridge by Craik, and so on. All these separate developments dealt with communicational problems, especially with the problem of what sort of thing is an organized system." Rumors of the strange perspectives of cybernetics reached the general public, very often brought together with the new electronic computers ("giant electronic brains"), but its universal claims generated a certain reserve in academia. There was simply no place in the academic disciplines for such a vague field.

At the same time the growing use of data processing equipment demonstrated a substantial need for computer specialists on all levels of education. US-Universities reacted with the introduction of computer science, computer engineering, or information science courses and curricula, with ACM curricular recommendations starting in 1968. British universities followed and continental Europe introduced academic programming and systems engineering courses. Germany followed US-curricula, but took the name *Informatik* from the French *informatique*. As in other countries, *Informatik* prevented the possible academic career of cybernetics in West Germany, as there was no necessity to start two different but closely related disciplines.

2. CONSTRUCTING A NEW DISCIPLINE

2.1 Scientific Discussions – Political Decisions

It seems that Philippe Dreyfus introduced the name Informatique from the elements Information and Automatique or Éléctronique in 1962. It was used throughout the French press. After even *Le Monde* printed it, the *Académie Française* defined it officially in 1967: "*Science du traitement rationnel, notamment par machines automatiques, de l'information considérée comme le support des connaissances humaines et des communications dans les domaines technique, économique et social.*"

This definition shows its peculiarities. Most interesting, it assumes that the newly defined *informatique* is already a science. Its object is the rational treatment of information, especially with automatically working machines (i.e. computers). This science should support human knowledge and skills as well as communication. Applications of that treatment are to be found in technical, economical, and social domains. Clearly this definition looks far beyond programming and use of computers. It embeds hardware and software in a field of applications and connects it with human work and communication.

Many European languages adopted that word, though informatics has been used in the U.K. since 1967 as synonymous to information science. In (West-)Germany *Informatik* made a strange twist: While it uses the French word, it sticks firmly to the American usage of computer science (with elements from computer engineering). Computing machines are seen as the base of the newly formed discipline. Neither problems nor consequences of the rational treatment, i.e. rationalization of work force, nor the communicative aspects of the new technology are themes of the academic discipline. Technical problems and their mathematical foundations form the almost exclusive discourse in *Informatik*, while practical applications, as well as economics and social questions are generally left out. The new discipline started 1969 in Germany with federal funding for eighteen university working groups.

Wolfgang Giloi wrote 1969 in a pamphlet of the Technical University of Berlin: "It was obvious, right from the beginning, that the notion Informatik had to be synonymous with Computer Science, i.e., it should enclose approximately that, what is understood as Computer Science in the U.S.A." This referential definition unveils its recursive wit in the following sentence: "The problem one had to face there, was that in the U.S.A. there is no common and general understanding what this discipline should be."[1]

This non-definition shows clearly that the whole process of introducing the new discipline was not guided by the desire of precise definition. It was instead a matter of sciento-political cooperation between interested researchers who tried to establish an inner circle while excluding unwanted or presumably less important actors. *Informatik* was exactly what the members of the founding committees and the heads of the new departments and chairs did or intended to do. And this was deeply rooted in mathematics and electronic engineering. Important applications like business data processing were left out. The whole definition process of the discipline was much more a social selection than a scientific distinction.

2.2 Politics of Choice and Exclusion

Explicit definitions of the term "Informatik" were rarely given in the first years (perhaps with the notable exception of Heinz Zemanek's paper from 1971), and there was certainly no generally accepted common definition. But there is a common attitude in all definitions of the newly founded discipline: They all draw lines of distinction to the manifold of other emerging or

[1] As an additional note on confusion it should be mentioned that the Technical University of Berlin founded its Computer Science department under the name "Fachbereich Kybernetik."

competing sciences, like cybernetics, semiotics, numerical mathematics and instrumental mathematics, formal logic and theory of computation, control theory, business data processing, operations research, system theory, information theory, coding theory, cryptography, game theory, semiconductor technology and (micro-) electronics, memory and storage technology, but also process automation, communication theory, and bionics. They were either excluded or thought to play only a marginal role in informatics – perhaps with the exception of formal logic and computation theory. The definition of the discipline was done primarily by exclusion. It seems that there was only one common sciento-political agreement among the founders of informatics, namely to become as independent as possible from the faculties they came from and where they found less resonance and cooperation than expected.

Of course, exclusion and distinction are necessary when something new is constructed. The process was however not driven by the inner necessities of the field, but primarily by political motives without much regard for the external demands, even when these were not unreasonable. Especially the hopes and demands of industry, finance companies and the public sector for academically educated data processing personnel, able to cope with the actual problems of information processing (including knowledge of COBOL and OS/360), were largely ignored in the academic field. As a result academic informatics generated an application gap quite beyond the unavoidable differences between practice and its scientific reflection. This application gap widened when many chairs in the newly founded discipline were given to academically trained mathematicians or engineers. Other fundamental aspects of system design and software construction like the study of organizations, teamwork, working conditions, psychology, economics, or application fields were generally ignored or considered to be less important. As a consequence methodological uncertainties show up wherever mathematical or logical foundations of informatics are insufficient to achieve a task. Though the application gap was recognized by many and often mourned, it is still not bridged.

2.3 Politics First: Cybernetics in East Germany

While the USSR was keen to copy US-successes in science and technology there was also some reserve to enter a common technological framework. This resulted in a series of publications on cybernetics, starting with a paper by Jaroschewskij (1952), denouncing its inhumane nature and the obscure and bourgeois character. About the same time Norbert Wiener (1950) wrote his book *The Human Use of Human Beings*, a pathetic pamphlet for a moderate modernization of production technology, deeply concerned about the influence of automation on employment and social balances. But his earlier verdict "Information is information, neither matter nor energy. No materialism which does not take this into account can survive the present day". was considered as an open attack to dialectical materialism. In addition his preference of feedback to deterministic cause-effect models and the mere thought of non-deterministic self-organization with possible political implications were additional offences to the Stalinistic understanding of scientific development. But these contrapositions were rarely found in engineering or natural science departments as the power of the new thoughts about control and computation were considered to be promising challenges.

Though this fight against a political philosophy of science may be seen as hard times for all contemporaries, it was only period of less than a decade, ending with the process of de-Stalinization. In 1957 Khinchin's book *Mathematical Foundations of Information Theory* was published and in 1958 a book by I.A. Poletajew *Signal* changed the Russian perception of the field – in parallel to the successful launch of the Sputnik. In 1962 Poletajew's book was translated to German with the more appropriate title *Kybernetik*. But there was also a vivid perception of western literature in the socialist countries – it was more a question of access than an ideology.

The most prominent protagonist for a Marxist interpretation of cybernetics was Georg Klaus, who chaired a research group on logic and epistemology at Humboldt-Universität in East-Berlin. He explained and defended the new cybernetic approaches in a series of books and articles. But even after his interventions the field with its fuzzy borders kept some "ideological haut-gôut" that remained despite the high esteem of its technical virtues in space and military. Under the verdict of demarcation the curricular introduction of *Informatik* was beyond reach in Eastern Germany. Instead *cybernetics* and *automatic control technology* were considered to open roads towards computerized planning and control. For a while, cybernetics was regarded higher in Eastern Germany than in the West, leading to some faculties that took these names.

3. HALF A CENTURY LATER ...

3.1 Informatik – Still in a State of Transition

Classification oscillates between submission and omnipotent phantasies, result of the "radical novelty" (Edsger Dijkstra) and the rapid development of the discipline and its underlying technology. It is obvious that the real definition of the discipline *Informatik* was chiefly done by academic practice, by teaching courses, by teaching manuals, by workshops, conferences, and research journals. It should be noted, however, that it was only occasionally influenced by practical data processing outside academic institutions. As a result *Informatik* is generally considered to be "theory" from the outside, whereas it is in fact the sum of academic practices, in which theoretical aspects are reduced to mathematical foundations.

Ironically, the newly founded German *Informatik*-departments were so successful in excluding suspicious looking and deviant content that they had to start with a bare minimum of lectures. The curricular plan developed by GAMM/NTG, which was adopted by nearly all faculties, filled only 18 hours per week (of a total of 80) in the first two academic years with genuine informational content and only 24 hours (of a total of 72) in the second two years. If the other disciplines would have been more tolerant they could have easily included the new discipline as a specialization.

But after a short warm-up period the discipline made many further distinctions and generated a plethora of new sub-fields. Already in 1985 it was no longer possible for the then more than 20 faculties to agree on a general scheme of practical informatics in the Bundesrepublik as demanded by the federal "Rahmenrichtlinien" (frame of reference). The discipline had entered its adolescence.

After becoming an academic discipline informatics went through a series of paradigmatic shifts. While computers started as automatic calculating devices their recognition changed completely with the advent of smaller and cheaper equipment, especially with PCs. Desktop applications like Wordstar, Dbase, or Visicalc made small computers a tool for office. With the enormous growth of computing power, main memory and auxiliary storage computers became multi-media machines with direct manipulation interfaces. Networked computers are universal media machines, demonstrating that all media, despite differences in origin and use, may be stored, processed, and distributed as binary numbers: An ongoing shift from the Gutenberg Galaxy towards a coming Turing Galaxy.

3.2 Cybernetics, Are You Still There?

Cybernetics underwent other paradigmatic shifts, from feedback loops to Heinz von Foerster's "second order" self-organization. Additional application areas fulfilled Norbert Wiener's prophetical subtitle - *Communication and Control in Animal and Machine* - moving cybernetic ideas into biology and sociology – in Germany under the influence of Niklas Luhmann. But cybernetics never reached the status of a self-contained discipline as it was in the case of computer science or Informatik. As a consequence the field as a whole went into agony. While informatics became an acceptable answer to a lack of academically educated workers since decades, the proponents of cybernetics hardly found a way to establish a field of study – with exceptions. There are still some magazines and congresses on cybernetics, and there are departments at the University of Magdeburg and the University of Stuttgart, though this faculty is part of the mechanics department, originating from control theory.

Why did cybernetics fail as a general academic endeavour? Probably its proponents aimed too high and too low at the same time, sometimes confusing even friendly supporters. Self-organization as second-order cybernetics is a really complex challenge, certainly beyond our actual technological possibilities and still not in the mainstream of deterministic technical thinking. As a practical approach beyond the laboratory, cybernetics aimed too low. Feed-back loops are a very narrow instrument compared to the plasticity of computer software.

But there is still an open question: Where is a general theoretical framework for computer science as the science of the information age?

REFERENCES AND RELATED LITERATURE

Bateson, Gregory, 1967, Cybernetic Explanation, *American Behavioral Scientist* 10, pp. 29-32.

Bauer, Friedrich L., 1974, Was heißt und was ist Informatik? Merkmale zur Orientierung über eine neue wissenschaftliche Disziplin, in: *IBM Nachrichten* Nr. 223, pp. 333-337

Bauer, Friedrich L.; Goos, Gerhard, 1970/71, *Informatik: Eine einführende Übersicht*, 2 Bde., 1. Aufl. Berlin, Heidelberg, New York; 2nd Ed. 1973/74; 3rd Ed. 1982/84; 4th Ed. 1990

Beer, Stafford, 1966, Kybernetik und Mangement, Frankfurt/Main: S.Fischer, 1966 (orig. Cybernetics and Management, London: English Universities Press, 1959)

Brauer, Wilfried; Haake, Wolfhart; Münch, Siegfried, 1973, *Studien- und Forschungsführer Informatik*, Bonn: GMD und Bad Godesberg: DAAD, 2nd Ed. 1974, 3rd Ed. 1978, 4th Ed. 1980

Brauer, Wilfired; Haake, Wolfhart; Münch, Siegfried, 1982, *Studien- und Forschungsführer Informatik*, 1. Aufl. Berlin, Heidelberg, New York, 2. Ed. 1989

Brauer, Wilfried; Münch, Siegfried, 1996, *Studien- und Forschungsführer Informatik*, 3. Ed. Berlin, Heidelberg, New York

Bundesminister für wissenschaftliche Forschung, 1968, Empfehlungen zur Ausbildung auf dem Gebiet der Datenverarbeitung, in: *Internationale Elektronische Rundsch*au 8, S.211

Communications of the ACM, 1989, A Debate on Teaching Computer Science, in: *CACM* 32:12, pp. 1397-1414

Coy, Wolfgang; Nake, Frieder; Pflüger, Jörg-Martin; Rolf, Arno; Siefkes, Dirk; Seetzen, Jürgen; Stransfeld, Reinhard. (Hrsg.), 1992, *Sichtweisen der Informatik*, Braunschweig, Wiesbaden: Vieweg

Couffignal, Louis, 1962, *Kybernetsiche Grundbegriffe*, Stuttgart: agis, (french orig. Les Notions des Bases, Paris: Gauthier-Villars)

Denning, Peter J.; Comer, Douglas E.; Gries, David e.a., 1989, Computing as a Discipline, in: *CACM* 32:1, pp. 9-23

Donth, Hans H., 1984, Der Aufbau der Informatik an Deutschen Hochschulen, in: *Elektronische Rechenanlagen* 26:5, pp. 223-228

Friedrich, Jürgen, Harro Schweizer, Eberhard Sens, 1975, *Marxismus und Kybernetik*, Kronberg/Ts.: Scriptor

Foerster, Heinz von (ed.), 1974, *Cybernetics of Cybernetics*. Biological Computer Laboratory, University of Illinois, Urbana, Illinois

GAMM/NTG, Stellungnahme zu den "Empfehlungen zur Ausbildung auf dem Gebiet der Datenverarbeitung" des BMF vom 20. 6. 1969

Giloi, Wolfgang K., 1970, Was ist Informatik?, in: TUB 2 1, pp. 4-15

Gries, David, 1991, Teaching Calculation and Discrimination: A more Effective Curriculum, in: *Communications of the ACM* 34 3, pp. 44-55

Hartmann, B., 1959, Die elektronische Datenverarbeitung in Lehre und Praxis. Ergebnisse einer Studienreise nach den USA, Berlin, Köln, Frankfurt a. M.

Jaroschewskij, M., 1952, Die Kybernetik – Eine 'neue Wissenschaft' der Obskuranten, *Neue Welt*, (russ. Orig. in Literaturnaja Gazetta, 5.4.1952)

Khinchin, A, 1957, *Mathematical Foundations of Information Theory*, Dover, New York.

Klaus, Georg, 1961, *Kybernetik aus philosophischer Sicht*, Berlin (DDR): Dietz

Klaus, Georg, 1969, *Kybernetik und Erkenntnistheorie*, Berlin (DDR): Deutscher Verlag der Wissenschaften

Klaus, Georg, 1973, *Kybernetik – eine neue Universalphilosophie der Gesellschaft?*, Berlin (DDR): Akademie-Verlag (Series: Zur Kritik der bürgerlichen Ideologie #27; ed. M. Buhr)

Kuhn, Thomas, 1962, *The Structure of Scientific Revolutions*, Chicago: University of Chicago Press

Möhring, Manfred, 1990, *Zur Frühgeschichte der Informatik in der DDR*, in: 1. Ribnitzer Informatikhistorisches Kolloquium (Rostocker Wissenschaftshistorische Manuskripte, H. 19), Universität Rostock, Sektion Geschichte, pp. 18-31

Naur, Peter, 1992, *Computing: A Human Activity*, New York, Reading, Mass.

Nora, Simon; Minc, Alain., 1978, *L'informatisation de la Societé*, Paris

Nygaard, Kristen, 1986, Programming as a social activity, in: Kugler (Hrsg.) *Information Processing '86*: Proceedings of the IFIP 10th World Computer Congress, Dublin, September 1-5, 1986, Amsterdam e.a.

Parnas, David, 1990, Education for Computer Professionals, in: *IEEE Computer* 23:1, pp. 17-22

Pflüger, Jörg-Martin, 1994, Informatik auf der Mauer, in: *Informatik Spektrum* 17:6, pp. 251-257

Pias, Claus (ed.), 2003, *Cybernetics | Kybernetik, The Macy-Conferences 1946-1953*, Band I, Reprint of the conferences originally edited by Heinz von Foerster 1949-1953, Zürich-Berlin: Diaphanes

Poletajew, I.A., 1964, *Kybernetik*, Berlin (DDR): VEB Deutscher Verlag der Wissenschaften, 1964 (russ. Orig. *Signal*, Moscow 1958)

Scharf, Joachim-Herrmann (Ed.), 1972, Deutsche Akademie der Naturforscher Leopoldina, *Informatik*, Proc. Jahresversammlung vom 14. bis 17. Oktober 1971 zu Halle (Saale), Leipzig

Schinzel , Britta (Ed.), 1996, *Schnittstellen – Zum Verhältnis von Informatik und Gesellschaft*, Braunschweig, Wiesbaden

Steinbuch, Karl, 1963, *Automat und Mensch*, Berlin-Heidelberg e.a.: Springer

Wilhelm, Reinhard.. 1996. *Informatik – Grundlagen, Anwendungen, Perspektiven*, München

Wiener, Norbert, 1948, *Cybernetics, or Control and Communication in the Animal and the Machine*. Paris: Hermann & Cie, Cambridge, Massachusetts: The Technology Press; New York: John Wiley & Sons, Inc.

Wiener, Norbert, 1950, *The Human Use of Human Beings*, Houghton Mifflin, Boston Mass.

Winograd, Terry; Flores, Fernando, 1986, *Understanding Computers and Cognition: a New Foundation for Design*, Norwood, N. J.

Zemanek, Heinz, 1971, Was ist Informatik?, in: *Elektronische Rechenanlagen* 13:4, pp. 157-161

Zemanek, Heinz, 1992, *Das geistige Umfeld der Informationstechnik*, Berlin, Heidelberg, New York: Springer

GOVERNMENT SPONSORED OPEN SOURCE SOFTWARE FOR SCHOOL EDUCATION

Andrew E. Fluck
University of Tasmania, Australia
E-mail: Andrew.Fluck@utas.edu.au

Abstract: The history of computing can be seen in terms of cultural change engendered by philosophical opposition. In education some key philosophical dichotomies are those of commercial-copyright versus free open source software, and office-centric pedagogies versus rich software libraries to support the whole school curriculum. The 'Blue File' software library was generated by four centres supporting students with special learning needs in Britain in the early 1980s, and embodied important features relevant to these tensions. More recently a longitudinal study in Tasmania has provided data to take the story further, highlighting the dangers of an office-centric approach to ICT in school education. The paper concludes with an argument for the exploration of online learning objects as a possible teacher-friendly solution to providing teachers with a rich repertoire of curriculum-focused learning activities.

Key words: Free source software; Open source software; School education; On-line learning objects; Office productivity software.

1. INTRODUCTION

The history of computing is rather like that of nations: a continuous series of battles arising from differences of belief. This paper concentrates on two entwined differences of philosophy. The first is the battle between proprietary and open standards. The second is the battle between office-centric conceptualisations of ICT in school education and the power of rich libraries of curriculum-focused software. The outcome of these battles has a great deal to tell us about management of a change process that requires and will enact fundamental cultural shifts.

2. GOVERNMENT-SPONSORED SOFTWARE

In the early 1980s the British government supported the introduction of ICT into schools by subsidising their purchase of the endemic BBC microcomputer. This model achieved export status and entered a second generation with the Archimedes range before obsolescence beneath the heels of the PC. Government support for educational software and teacher professional development was provided through the Micro-Electronics Programme that set up 14 regional centres for general education and four others to support children with special educational needs. These four SEMERCs (Special Education Micro-Electronics Resource Centres) were managed by Bob Dyke/Martin Littler (Manchester); Jean Tait/Andrew Fluck (Redbridge, London); Jean Johnston (Bristol) and Colin Richards/Derek Cooper (Newcastle). They were established in 1984 under the auspices of the Council for Educational Technology with Mary Hope as national co-ordinator (Jean Johnston in Vincent, 1989, p.276 & Saunders, 1984, p.95). Most were closed in 1989.

These four centres were responsible for the development of a range of software that was freely copyable, called 'The Blue File'. The writing of this software was promoted by encouraging and sharing ideas between teachers, commissioning programmers to implement software suggestions, providing release time for teachers to write programs themselves and by centre staff taking on all these roles. This range of software was primarily intended to be used by children with special educational needs. The programs therefore addressed basic skills such as matching, selecting, simple numeracy, switch-operated communication etc. Making the programs simple to operate for these students yet catering for a range of input methods to enable those with physical disabilities to use the software, represented a real challenge. Some of the most advanced technologies of the time were utilised to address these difficulties. Input devices such as the expanded keyboard, the photonic wand (a light-pen equipped with a small telescope was mounted on one arm of some eye-glasses), touch screens, all kinds of switches, and in particular the Concept Keyboard, were used. This latter was a touch sensitive tablet upon which a sheet of paper could be placed carrying pictures or icons representing elements of a learning situation. When connected to a simple word processor, students could write sentences by merely touching pictures or phrases on the paper as it rested upon the concept keyboard. Output devices such as robotic devices, turtles, musical instruments and voice synthesizers were also employed.

Some of the key aspects of this software are recognised as important today, such as their framework or content-free nature, the customisability of tools and toolbars, and the capacity to adapt to user-defined input devices.

This was recognised as vital to accommodate the range of intellectual and physical abilities of the children with special needs, and this kind of accessibility is now built into operating systems. Another important aspect of this software library was its breadth of curriculum coverage, offering simulated canal locks, activities to teach life skills and tools to promote literacy through interactive scene construction.

The 'Blue File' programs were freely copyable for educational use in the United Kingdom and were distributed around the world, even in Western Australia (Morgan, 1990 ,p.14). Most were for the Acorn BBC computer, but many were later transferred to the PC platform. Over thirty titles became available, as described in Table 1.

Table 1. Blue File software descriptions

Title	*Description*
Acorn Speech programs	Six simple programs incorporating spoken instructions from the voice output hardware.
Annual Review System	Database for tracking individual students through personal curriculum plans.
Beans on Toast	A sequencing simulation for cooking a meal using a gas cooker with rich graphics and animations.
Belmont Programs	Nine programs covering colouring, matching, money and sequencing for children with severe learning difficulties.
Berkshire Catalogue	Software database which indexes programs according to their curriculum area and age level.
Brian Apter programs	Visual stimulus programs for young switch users.
Compact 1+2+3	These programs aim to stimulate language by giving a wide range of simplified scenes controlled by switches, the keyboard or the concept keyboard.
Driver	Simulation of driving a car, using the concept keyboard as an input device for the steering wheel, gear stick and foot control pedals.
Early Fingers	Targeting etc using a multiple-point infra red scanning touch screen from the Spastic Society. The programs feature animated cats and mice and cover sequencing, targeting, tracking, early number concepts and painting.
ECL	A collection of software for the Tandy book and concept keyboard on counting, measuring and matching.
Eresby software	Multiple input device programs (QWERTY or concept touch sensitive keyboards, or sound sensitive micromike) on dressing, counting, memory, and drawing.

Title	*Description*
Firs	Early learning material covering counting, subtraction, coins, sorting words and for preparing arithmetic worksheets.
Floor Robots	Pre-LOGO activities controlling a turtle using joysticks, microphones and other devices.
Inner City	For reinforcing basic skills in primary and special schools, with several simple adventure games.
Lists	Jargon-free database for very young children to explore categories of self-concept.
Look & Think	For visually handicapped youngsters.
Magic Seeker	This contains a set of data files and overlays to go with a range of content-free software such as Prompt, Touch Explorer and Lists, concentrating on the concept of a magical journey of discovery.
MAISE programs	Eight programs covering counting, words and shape-matching.
Picture	An early pre-number game for young children with severe learning difficulties, linking the screen display with pictures on the concept keyboard.
Moving In	A simulation of unloading a removal van full of furniture into a house. Control is through creating grammatically correct sentences using QWERTY or concept keyboard.
Picture Play	Picture-making activities using a range of input devices.
Prepositions	Practices the use of prepositions (in, by, beside, underneath, behind etc) with simple animation effects.
Programmer's Toolkits 1 & 2	Early utilities for freezing processor activity to facilitate screenshot capture and printout. Also includes routines for image compression.
Prompt 2 & 3	Flexible and popular assistive word-processor which allows students to use the QWERTY or concept keyboard to input text.
Redfile 1 & 2	Weaving simulation, building sentences by numbers, visual stimulus, early number and attention span software using single switch or keyboard input.
Simple use of language	The antics of Fred the fly: this figure is animated to practice use of nouns, adjectives and prepositions.
Single Switch Trainer & Wiper	These two programs enable a child using a single switch to learn how to gain control with it, building up a scene.
Sums	Drill and practice software for exercise on the four rules of number. Problems are generated automatically at set levels of ability, and help/explanation is available at every stage.
Touch Explorer	Classic content free software for concept keyboard touch-sensitive pad. Teachers can link pictures or real objects to text and voices.

Title	*Description*
West Midlands	Early learning programs.
Wordsearcher	Enables children to build their own simple word-puzzles and have the printouts in double-height characters.

Learning to Cope, 1986/7

3. OPEN VERSUS PROPRIETARY STANDARDS

In retrospective review this range of government-sponsored software was critical to the adoption of information and communication technology (ICT) in not just special education but the broader school education community. One example can be drawn from the first version of the National Curriculum for England which suggested students should be able to "construct a simple story as a sequence of words pictures or sounds using an overlay keyboard or mouse" (HMSO, 1990, p.45). Eight years later the training standards for teachers required them to know the characteristics of talking word processors (Department for Education and Employment, 1998) an early example of which had been pioneered in the 'Blue File' software. These examples of non-traditional input and output systems were only one aspect which continued in later educational practice. Another was the way in which much of the best software was designed to be content-free or 'framework' in nature and could therefore be applied in many subject areas through the provision of appropriate data files. These data files could be devised with teaching materials by third parties and disseminated through educational exchanges. The critical factor here was the open nature of the standards for the files enabling anyone interested to construct new learning examples.

The battle between proprietary and open standards has almost invariably been won by the latter. The government-sponsored BBC computer in Britain and other countries lost out to the PC platform. The X400 OSI standards for email addresses and directories lost out to the Internet Engineering Taskforce's RFC 451 standards. Applebe (2003) predicts that Microsoft having adopted open XML for underlying file standards may shortly lose out in the competition with Linux and Open Office. Richard Stallman has argued since 1984 that the term 'free software' should be used and wrote the GPL (General Public Licence) to make the conditions clear. Linus Torvalds released the Linux operating system on 17th September 1991 under a modified version of the GPL (Rivlin, 2003, p.206). The 'Blue File' software pioneered this approach in the context of school education and achieved global impact.

4. OFFICE-CENTRIC VERSUS LIBRARIES OF CURRICULUM SOFTWARE

The nature of classroom computer use in more recent years bears comparison with the strategies embedded in the 'Blue File'. A seven-year longitudinal study of computer use in Tasmanian primary classrooms revealed a disturbingly monotonous classroom software diet. Using categories established by a national discussion process (Fluck, 1998) observations were made by over a hundred pre-service teachers each year to assess which of these categories were used by pupils in the classes they observed over at least a two week period. Publishing electronically or to paper was found in a steadily increasing proportion of classrooms. However, personal communications and problem solving remain restricted to a small fraction of these same classrooms (Table 2).

Table 2. Proportions of primary school classrooms where pupils were observed using computers in identified learning modes

Year	Publishing	Problem Solving	Independent Learning	Researching	Communicating
1995	75%	35%	36%	18%	6%
1996	78%	63%	44%	37%	11%
1997	82%	51%	52%	48%	16%
2000	86%	34%	59%	45%	35%
2001	85%	38%	50%	62%	42%
2002	86%	41%	66%	59%	39%
2003	94%	34%	72%	70%	42%

The results illustrate a trend to concentrate computer use in schools to the few basic software applications with which the teacher is familiar. This is often used to replicate activities that previously existed in the curriculum making ICT (where infrastructure is unreliable) a headache rather than an essential. This trend away from a rich repertoire of curriculum based software towards learning restricted by exclusive use of a basic 'Office' suite of productivity software can be seen as restrictive. It may satisfy a pedagogical rationale to prepare pupils for the world of work but does not easily translate into better learning in the wide range of subjects studied at school.

5. CONCLUSION

If ICT is to transform the curriculum then teachers need a rich library of software, either through open sources or from good collections of on-line learning objects. Open source projects in Australia include BELTS (Basic E-Learning Tool Set) sponsored by the government as a free open source software project to trial the use of on-line learning objects, and Moodle, an educational course management system used extensively in Western Australia (Oliver, 2003). Both of these can be found in Sourceforge.net, which hosts over 65,000 collaborative software projects (Goetz, 2003, p 166). The open source method has been applied to other joint ventures involving volunteers. Project Gutenberg uses distributed proof-reading whereby many copy editors check copyright-free texts for accuracy prior to dissemination (Goetz, 2003, p 166). The open source on-line encyclopedia 'Wikipedia' was designed using open source web-design software called Wiki by Jimmy Wales and his team from 2001. It had 150,000 entries, and hits to its web-site surpassed those of the Encyclopedia Britannica in 2003 (Goetz, 2003, p 166). The government education department for the state of Victoria in Australia sponsored a competition for school students to submit open source educational software (Wide Open Source, 2003), demonstrating a commitment to spreading the concepts through the education of students.

The Learning Federation <http://www.thelearningfederation.edu.au> is a joint venture involving government agencies which is developing a range of on-line learning objects for Australia and New Zealand. It is not the current intention of the Learning Federation to release its learning objects as open source code, reflecting the high cost of production. It remains to be seen what value these objects have as a market becomes established for such content. Characteristics of such a market may include language and cultural localization, and it will be important to link each object with appropriate points in the customer's school curriculum. As on-line learning objects become more widely available, they demonstrate the importance of the 'Blue File' concept of framework software, where different data files are accessed to provide learning experiences for different subject areas. However, the web-browser and plug-ins used to access the learning objects do not appear to be as flexible in terms of input and output device range as the 'Blue File' software showed possible.

REFERENCES

Applebe, W., 2003, The future of open source software, *J. of research and practice in IT*, **35**:4. On-line at http://www.acs.org.au/JRPITVolumes/JRPIT35/JRPIT35.4.227.pdf.

Department for Education and Employment, UK, 1998, *Summary of circular 4/98: Requirements for courses of initial teacher training*. Author: London, England. On-line at http://www.dfee.gov.uk/circulars/4_98/summary.htm on 5th June 2000.

Fluck, A., 1998, The KITOs - Key information technology outcomes for school students. *Australian Conference on Computers in Education*: Adelaide, Aust. On-line at http://cegsa.sa.edu.au/conference/acec98/papers/p_fluck.html

Goetz, T., 2003, Open source everywhere, *Wired*, November, pp. 158-208.

HMSO, 1990, *Technology in the National Curriculum*, HMSO, UK: Department of Education and Science and the Welsh Office.

Learning to Cope 1986/7. Educational Computing Ltd/EMAP: London, England.

Morgan, L., 1990, *Resource and Software Directory 1990*. L. Morgan: Melbourne, Australia.

Oliver, Nick, 2003, *Open source software in education*. Canberra Schools Linux User group. On-line at http://www.linux.act.edu.au/aeuopen/aeuopensource.html

Rivlin, Gary, 2003, Leader of the free world. *Wired*, November, 152-157 & 204-208., Saunders, Peter, 1984, *Micros for handicapped users*. Helena Press: Whitby, England.

Vincent, A. T., (Ed.), 1989, *New Technology, Disability and Special Educational Needs: some case studies*. Empathy Ltd c/o Hereward College of Further Education for the Open University and the Further Education Unit: Coventry, England.

Wide Open Source, 2003, *Wide open code: The open source Victoria scholar challenge*. On-line at http://www.osv.org.au/index.cgi?tid=6

LEARNING WITH THE ARTIFICIAL SCIENCES
A Paradigmatic Shift

Colin T. Schmidt, Philippe Cottier, and Christophe Choquet
Le Mans University, France
E-mail: Colin.Schmidt@univ-lemans.fr; Philippe.Cottier@univ-lemans.fr; Christophe.Choquet@univ-lemans.fr

Abstract: In what follows, we look into the intellectual history of Distance Education. We study the *methodological, political* and *epistemological* aspects of the shift of paradigms in the scientific thought used to construct distance learning objects. A global (not meaning exhaustive) coverage of the various ways in which instructional communication has been mediated is given. We consider e-learning's objects to be socio-technical in nature and thus that their history stems from the very beginnings of Artificial Intelligence.

Key words: Change; Artificial Intelligence; Policy Writing; CSCL; Otherhood

1. INTRODUCTION

According to P. Moeglin (2000), expert on cultural industrialisation and the computerisation of society at a Parisian University, we have totally lost track of the objects we learned with in the past, and more generally, communication in education. This has had its long-term consequences in Science: "the fragmentation and differentiation of sciences in the 20th century have reached a point where specialists working in different areas of what used to be a unified field of science no longer understand one another" (Kinelev 2003). Moeglin wonders: "what were the precursors to our present multimedia learning techniques?" We shall argue that the early technologies that sprang from Man's thought at the intersection of mathematics, physically manipulating objects, and human intelligence itself constitute the foundations of today's new world of education. What is the nature of these obsolete educational entities and how might they influence current research in the science of Distance Learning? Whatever the means might have been the problem in any pedagogical activity is to instill in one's students the *will* to acquire knowledge and thus the *desire* to communicate. The effectiveness of problem-solving is the main factor in the appraisal of progress in any science. In the same grain of thought, L. Laudan (1977) points out that it is important to explore the *intellectual history* of a domain of thought for two reasons, to write sound history and to make rational choices. The intellectual history of Artificial Intelligence (AI) — the core area of research used in modern Distance Learning — must be a "non-eliminable ingredient" in choosing between alternative actions for future work in such uses of AI.

Though computers are not the only technical objects we learn with, our intention here is not to establish an exhaustive history but to concentrate on the aspects having to do with the automation of Man's intellect and the methodology of evaluating distance learning systems. Even since the beginning of the new millennium, there have been quite a few changes in the role computing has had in educating people. Despite its trials and tribulations, more people are accepting this mode of learning. So be it. But when comparing with the precursors of 15-25 years ago we feel right at home in speaking about a paradigmatic shift in the use of Machine-Assisted Learning. Today, it would seem that Open and Distance Learning communities have allowed "libertarian pedagogical attitudes" to flourish. Up until the very end of the 20th century, studies concentrating on the relationship between humans and machines would check up on the *effects* of the demands of the public on the institution or on the *effects* of computers on individuals. But studying these well-defined activities is no longer *à la mode*. Why not?

2. SOME HISTORICAL BEGINNINGS OF DISTANCE LEARNING

In order to answer this and other questions, we will need to establish an historical setting and talk about some of the personalities involved in Artificial Intelligence, education, and related fields. Kinelev (2003) and Moeglin (2000) recall that the coming of printing to educational institutions was as great a revolution in teaching as was the advent of recent technologies like the Internet; one may attempt to say that Distance Education today only *makes use* of printing in a novel way; however that would be somewhat false as it also employs sound and images, a multimedia delivery which could well be calling out for multi-modal definitions of optimal learning activity and what the word "literacy" should now really mean.

Instructional radio and television were little more than simple reproductions of "boring" professors giving a lecture. Despite the failure of radio (1930s) to become a noticeable precursor to modern Distance Education, television gathered 400,000 students in 6500 public school classrooms in and around Indiana thanks to the Midwest Program on Airborne Television Instruction (MPATI) of the Ford Foundation (1960s); later spin-offs of this were Educational Television (ETV), Closed Circuit Television (CCTV) and Instructional Fixed Television Service (ITFS). In the late 1960s, Universities started reaching out to both on-campus and off-campus populations (Jeffreys, 2004).

As few people knew about computers then, speaking about the idea of converging television and computers would certainly have seemed a preposterous thing to do. But the Internet did come to be, and we could state that one of the prototypical versions of it was Campus Wide Information Systems — "online repositories for public-domain information generated on university campuses" (CBI). In the 1980s and 1990s the CWIS was envisioned as an information space where university students, faculty, and staff could engage in electronic self-publishing, retrieval of course information, and have access to e-mail, online library catalogue facilities, the campus phone book, and other remote facilities. [...] Credit for the earliest CWIS is usually given to CUinfo, deployed on October 10, 1982, by Steven L. Worona and others on an IBM mainframe." The information contained therein had the goal of encouraging uniformity and the building of inter-collegiate information system relationships but was "invariably obsolete even before reaching its users' hands". It did not really represent education but it is an important precursor to modern *textual* information flow within educational institutions (intranet/extranet).

Well before the early CWIS history, Martiel Vivet was already into more advanced educational content in down-to-earth situations. Vivet (later known for his "pedagogical micro-robotics") was one of the pioneers in using technology for genuine learning in industrial settings. His struggle to obtain the appropriate computing equipment and bring mathematics teachers in France to recognise the merits of automatically demonstrating theorems and the inherent pedagogical problem-solving nightmares that produced preliminary thinking material for his later experiences with employees in micro-worlds that needed training (Vivet, 2000). The "battle" with the mathematics teachers corresponds to the period between his discovery of the experiences in High Schools using wooden computers for students to study the effects on students' acquisition processes and that of Papert's LOGO, thus between 1973 and 1977. LOGO enabled Vivet to demonstrate the pedagogical merits of manipulating objects at a distance. We are convinced he put the spotlight on the difficulty in many problem-solving situations:

their resolution is first fully conceptual, which hinders the planning of actions as one has trouble 'seeing' the real world deployment, extension or it's application. Vivet seemed to be drawing nigh to Dreyfus' position in *What Computers Still Can't Do* (1972) that software, not having (human) corporal existence, needs to convey one if it is to help us understand what the computer is actually doing. Vivet demonstrated that, by using real physical objects, actions, and environments, or by representing them at a distance, learning becomes easier.

Another major pioneer in the field was J. Self, known for his "automatic teaching" in the late 1970s and his student modeling for Intelligent Tutor Systems (ITS) in the late 1980s. Going from automatic teaching to student modeling constitutes a major shift in focus. His ambition was to escape from the empiricism of ITS research by admitting that the building of an ITS system that works implies adopting a theoretical stance taking into account the fact that knowledge cannot be treated as information (Self, 1990). His life-long 'slide' from the computational towards the concerns in Educational Sciences influenced a domain of study that shifted from machine-centred to human-centred design. As other informed writers in the mid 1990s, he wrote simply of AI *in* education and no longer of education in AI.

In mentioning "libertarian pedagogical attitudes" earlier, we meant that with computer networks for learning the in-class learning process is not only vanishing, but learning is becoming less *teacher-driven* as there is no physical classroom in which to *'contain'* students. *Activity-directed study* has enabled giving more consideration to self-initiated action on the part of the student. In exploring the various stages involved in acquiring this, we wish to establish a prospective epistemology meant to encapsulate the redefinition process with regards to suitable learning procedures for the current workforce and to envisage renewing the meaning of what it means to be literate/illiterate. This is all the more necessary in a field that has barely identified itself (Shale, 1988). There are really three aspects to the paradigmatic shift we wish to discuss. In this sense, we could even speak about *three* paradigmatic shift*s*, namely methodological (Shift no. 1), political (Shift no. 2) and epistemological (Shift no. 3).

3. SHIFT NO 1: METHODOLOGY FOR ANALYSIS AND EVALUATION OF THE EXISTING

Computer-mediated distance learning as we know it today has existed for about a quarter of a century. In the early days, the community focused on the best possible computerisation of the system with an aim to *replacing* the teacher, as can be done with television. This initial approach had limited success. Little by little, the community started to reintegrate the (human) individual into the heart of the system. From simply technically-oriented, the system became "socio-technical", and the goal has shifted from replacing human activity to *assisting* human activity. A major reason for the methodological paradigmatic shift in question is the social acceptance of the World Wide Web. Its appropriation allows users with their own technical and cognitive skills to make the step towards using computerised learning environments. It would thus seem that the birth of the Internet has rendered e-learning tools familiar for transforming the nature of interactions from *1*/person-machine to *2*/person(s)-person(s) with, and through, machines.

Knowing what the user is doing with the machine is compulsory to studying the effects of the machine. J. Self's experience shows that we have been leading the learner away from the heuristic self-initiated learning of the past to contexts in which learning becomes a full-fledged social activity (1995). The knowledge being handled in the former situation was static (*objectivism)*, and in the latter situation, it is becoming increasingly dynamic. The "paradigmatic appellations" that J. Self assigns here are *constructivism* or even *situationism* (1995). Others would say that we have entered the era of *interactionism* (Caelen, 2003) in which the likeness of artificial and natural agents play similar — or even identical — roles in communication. Current learning tools being developed and tested include neo-ITS, Computer-supported Collaborative Learning (CSCL), Dialogue Systems (D. Luzzati *et al*, 1992) and Collective Activities in a Learning Context (CALC, *cf.* P. Tchounikine *et al*, 2003). This latter type of application *environment* merely provides the learner with a whole line of communication spaces and a complete toolbox for learning. Its advocates purposefully to use this *minimalist directivity* to encourage learner integration into group projects.

Obviously, accessibility to information catapulted distance education into a new age, but the appropriation of technologies by society can be accelerated if we learn about the needs of a learning group. Getting to know the user and his needs, or having an idea of what he is doing is not always possible with today's lesser defined learning activities. Inversely, we have to be able to predict the use of certain techniques on the computing side of the equation. The advancement of computing techniques also yields many combinations of tools in CALC learning environments. The first corroboration we could make between the technological and sociological dimensions concerned is that the causal-type analysis of the *behaviourist project* has taken a huge blow. As a matter of fact, it has been watered down to mere theoretical posturing on the impact of machines on society and *vice versa.*

E-learning research evolved in light of the results obtained. The effects linked to the functional vision of the machine slowly gave way to the difficulty of isolating variables in a causal relation. The question that is now leading the investigation is epidemiological in nature. What are learners really doing within their learning environment? Of the many devices they have at hand for learning, which ones are they using and how? And thus, on the technology side of the relationship, which types of tools are being promoted by developers and why? Our historical analysis up to the introduction of CALCs paints the context in which pedagogical diversification has since set in. Help menus, FAQs, chats, forums etc. and other generally good "excuses-for-not-getting-down-to-it" have been integrated into the task of learning *because* we wanted learning to become collective once again. We believe that the theoretical evolutions in the use of computers in education and their methodological implications come from society's propensity to learn differently in different epochs.

Qualifying group experience is becoming urgent. When one looks at the process starting in the 1970s, it is clear that there has been a general paradigmatic swing from "hey, look at what the computer can do!" to "what is the learner up to?" The question of the proper methodological analysis to employ must account for the socio-technical configuration of the system and work towards one that is optimal for the learning community. The fact that we currently use computerised group learning environments shows that we should not rely on causal analysis approaches any longer — those aimed at measuring single learners' performances — especially when using CALCs.

4. SHIFT NO. 2: DECISION-MAKING PROCESSES FOR COMPUTERISATION

In 1995 J. Self asked questions about the nature of knowledge that presuppose an operational definition of computer literacy. He also states that, over and beyond AI in Education's goal to promote computerisation in the knowledge society, it should have "broader aims: to develop ethical and moral values, to improve attitudes, to nurture better citizens, and so on". He might have been indicating a general societal problem linked to education itself.

Could there be something wrong with State-prescribed learning programmes? People do not only wish to have more control over *how* they learn but *what* they learn. They have had a taste of *direct control* with the Internet, i.e. serendipity, or the educational virtue found in freely wondering from text to text as pointed out by S. Papert (1993) of the MIT *Epistemology and Learning Group*. This opens the doors to change which means breaking away from the traditional institutional values of learning, but this change is slow in coming. Papert writes about the *design of school* and states that "the possibility of freely exploring worlds of knowledge calls into question the very idea of an administered curriculum" (a typically strong American proposition). *Literacy for all* types of programmes have generally implied reading, writing, and arithmetic; but the new surge, with the help of computers, multimedia applications and networks should eventually modify the very definition of literacy. Vladimir Kinelev recently spoke of creating a new educational content to combat anti-individualistic attitudes and of the necessity of *New Literacy* due to new social demands and the new world around us, without really being able to say what "New Literacy" meant (*cf.* the UNESCO Summit, December 2003). Nonetheless, his idea of promoting transversal educational content by putting the emphasis on the less materially specialised disciplines (History, Arts, Law, Philosophy, etc.) in order to enhance the social nature of the human being and augment the inner balance of the individual comes as a change in attitude ten years after Papert accused the pundits of the *Educational Establishment* of not wanting to recognise the consequences of the progress of technology.

The big corporate players in America followed by those in England were the first to understand both that technology was sprinting ahead and that there was an important need for the internal e-learning training for their employees. Starting in the late 1980s with Motorola University (MU) in the United States, Lloyds Bank, Hilton Hotels, Rolls-Royce and IBM used "trained career coaches" to help employees establish their own "clear career progression pathways". A form of "watched freedom" that represents *direct control* nonetheless. The public services are catching onto the idea now: Arizona Government University (AzGU), British Telecom Academy (2001) and the National Health Service University (NHSU, 2004) just to mention a few, the last of which will be the largest in England (Cottee, 2003). In France, the National Centre for Distance Education (CNED) has been highly implicated along with the Ministry of Education in developing e-learning in the public sector with the creation of "digital campuses" (CNED, 2002).

Although it would be to the detriment of mastering reading etc., combat anti-individualistic attitudes could be a good pretext to adapt the recent proposals from the AI community, that is to increase development of learning through (multi-player) *game-playing techniques*. For the time being, this approach has a rather commercial flavour as it targets high-level corporate decision-makers, but we feel it is worth public assessment procedures as it does encourage the remedy of socialising.

Look at the historical process of innovations coming to support Distance Learning. We went from audio text flow on the radio (failure) through TV — mainly visual and audio text flow (success) — to multimedia multi-text convergence, meaning visual, audio, plain text plus animations, etc. (strong technical integrative progress and very high acceptance). What has this to say about the nature of the instructional text today? And the type of literacy we are demanding of our students? There are perhaps other changes not too far down the road.

5. SHIFT NO. 3: AI AND THE IDENTITY OF THE LEARNER

Hard AI constitutes the earliest plausible premise for ITS, CSCL and CALC. The diverse aspects of Herbert Simon's intellectual life may have been meant to come together to form 3rd Millennium Distance Education. In any event, he was a "heavy-better" with his 'big' predictions. The period of 1952 to 1958 was a fast one for H. Simon: he met A. Newell at the Rand Corporation in Santa Monica California and focused his attention on the theory of games; in August 1956 he automated, along with Shaw and Newell, the very first theorem proving process using an example from Whitehead & Russell's *Principia Mathematica*; he studied A. de Groot's theories on the psychology of chess playing (Gobet, 2002) and, by 1958, Newell, Shaw and Simon had written the first computer program to play chess. In his 1958 *Operations Research* article with Newell, he predicted that in ten years time a computer would become the world chess champion. This did not happen actually until 40 years later.

While waiting for the triumph of IBM's *Deep Blue* over Kasparov in 1997, IA diversified. In the 70s, R. Schank was implementing "scripts" — frames for stereotypical social activities — to manipulate language in special purpose micro-worlds to deal with common sense knowledge (i.e. ordering food in a restaurant). However, the goal was still like that of Simon's, *teaching machines to "reason" like humans*; one could say his scripts described game-world scenarios. Presently, the quick evolution of work on pre-set fictive situations has caused important AI figures to climb back on the game-playing band-wagon. In the Introduction to Prensky's book (2001), one will notice that Papert goes along with this idea, though he would have done so already in 1993 (*cf.* Shift no. 2). And Schank's 35 year-long endeavours in prescriptive scenarisation have also been reconverted over to... yes, Distance Learning through Playing Games (2002).

Today's workforce is changing due to the ubiquitous nature of the digital. The idea in this new "*ludic AI* for acquisition purposes" is to make use of the newer non-conformist mind-sets we find in liberal enterprise in a lucrative way. Company CEO's are unaccustomed to the nature of the skills and knowledge of today's youth as they do not generally have a high literacy rate —according to the traditional definition. Human Resource managers have nevertheless realised they present the specific potential of becoming the future strategy-builders of their firms. Could the current emphasis of turning corporate e-learning environments into tools for socialisation and fun be due to Simon? He was involved in administrative behaviour, decision-making, human psychology and the first game-playing applications of AI. He was known for saying "play with your knowledge and explore the unexpected connections". Even if he did make his own unexpected connection on the *ampleur* games would attain in distance education and 'forget' to make the prediction, AI as the foundation of e-learning owes a lot to his advancing knowledge in a topic of interest that has stimulated research for half a century.

6. CONCLUSION

In light of these three shifts in the history of computers in education, future perspectives in this young field of research should focus on inter-learner relations now that learning whilst exploring Otherhood has become paramount. The first shift shows that it has become blatantly impossible to link all the effects to their corresponding causes in high-functionality environments; new methods are necessary for CSCL applications (*cf.* Cottier & Schmidt). The second shift demonstrates that new dynamism in promoting transversal knowledge acquisition has found a place in international policy writing. One question may rest unanswered for the reader, particularly with respect to the third shift. Can we maintain the idea of paradigmatic shift if playing games started and ended the historical process of the AI Sciences in education? Or has AI taken us round full swing from chess-playing through emulating serious-toned courses on the Internet and back to playful activities in virtual classes (i.e. two shifts)? We believe we can maintain it because there is a fundamental issue when it comes to the pedagogical objective: *who* is acquiring the knowledge? *Humans teaching machines to play games has given way to using networked machines to teach humans*. But this should not come as a surprise as, halfway down the road to the New Millennium Distance Education initiatives discussed herein, a Socio-Psychologist from Harvard sent out a "tremor signal" to specialists in AI trying to teach machines to 'think'. In speaking of the computer's physical opacity in 1984, S. Turkle states that "the computer brings out thinking more than it determines it. […] The computer has become 'an object we think with'". This corresponds roughly to the period of the beginnings of ITS. Since then, we have learned to think *through* this technical object in order to play and communicate with others. And most importantly, since the days of radio- and television-supported distance learning, our intellectual history has taught us that, whatever the distance, learning must be made fun.

REFERENCES

Bruillard, E., Delozanne, E., Leroux, P., Delannoy P., Dubourg X. Jacoboni P., Lehuen J., Luzzati, D. & Teutsch, P., 2000, "Quinze ans de recherche informatique sur les sciences et techniques éducatives au LIUM", *Sciences et techniques éducatives*, Vol. 7, n° 1, p. 87-145.

Centre for the History of Information Technology, *Charles Babbage Institute(CBI)*, http://www.cbi.umn.edu/ .

CNED, 2002. Campus numériques, enjeux et perspectives pour la formation ouverte et à distance. Rapport de mission sous la direction Michel Averous et Gilbert Touzot, Editions Cned. http://www.cned.fr/Etablissement/organisation/campusnumeriques/ enjeux.pdf

Caelen, J., "Systèmes interactifs", in Miège, B., 2003, *Communication personnes-systèmes informationnel. Traité des sciences et techniques de l'information*, Paris: Hermès/Lavoisier.

Cottee, P., 2003, "Workplace Wisdom. Corporate or virtual universities are the clever way to meet training needs", *Guardian Weekly*, October 30th, p. 26.

Cottier, P. & Schmidt, C.T. (forthcoming), "Dialogue in context, Towards a Referential Approach in Collective Learning".

de Groot, A.D., 1965. *Thought and Choice in Chess*, The Hague: Mouton.

Dreyfus, H., 1972. *What Computers* Still *Can't Do: A Critique of Artificial Reason*, (1994, Fourth printing) Cambridge, MA: The MIT Press.

Gobet, F., 2002, "Travailler avec Herbert Simon", Revue des sciences et technologies de l'information, série *Revue d'intelligence artificielle*, Special Issue "Représentations, découverte et rationnalité. Hommage à Herbert Simon", Hermès/Lavoisier, p. 29-37.

Gobet, F., 2002, "Recherche et reconnaissance de patterns chez les experts", Revue des sciences et technologies de l'information, série *Revue d'intelligence artificielle*, Special Issue "Représentations, découverte et rationnalité. Hommage à Herbert Simon", Hermès/Lavoisier, p. 165-190.

Jeffries, M., (15/01/2004), "The History of Distance Education", "Research in Distance Education" : www.Digitalschool.net/edu/DL_history_mJeffries.html .

Kinelev, V., 2003, "Education for Evolving Societies", *Proceedings of the 2003 World Summit on the Information Society*, Geneva 10-12 December, pp. 10-16.

Laudan, L., 1977, *Progress and its Problems. Towards a Theory of Scientific Growth*, Los Angeles: University of California Press.

Moeglin, P., 2000, "Du mode d'existence des outils pour apprendre", *Les Enjeux*, Grenoble, p. 4, www.u-grenoble3.fr/les_enjeux/ 2000Moeglin/home.html

Papert, S., 1993, "Obsolete Skill Set : The 3 Rs — Literacy and Letteracy in the Media Ages", *Wired Magazine*.

Pitrat, J., 2002, "Herbert Simon, pionnier de l'Intelligence Artificielle", Revue des sciences et technologies de l'information, série *Revue d'intelligence artificielle*, Special Issue "Représentations, découverte et rationnalité. Hommage à Herbert Simon", Hermès/Lavoisier, p. 11-16.

Prensky, M., 2001, *Digital Game Based Learning*, New York: McGraw-Hill.

Schank, R., 2002, *Designing World-Class E-Learning: How IBM, GE, Harvard Business School and Columbia University are Succeeding at E-Learning*, New York: McGraw-Hill.

Schank, R., 1975, "Using Knowledge to Understand" and "The Primitive Acts of Conceptual Dependency", *Theoretical Issues in Natural Language Processing*, Cambridge MA June 10-13.

Schmidt, C.T., (forthcoming), "An Epistemological Analysis of Artificial Intelligence in University Education".

Schmidt, C.T., (2004), "Should We Not Make Room for Non-persons in Artificial Intelligence?", *WCC-2004 AIAI*, Aug. 22-27, Toulouse, France.

Schmidt, C.T., & Ruch P., 1999, "Evolution of Man's Needs and Technological Progression: Pragmatic Foundations for a Relational Coupling", Chapter 16 *in* Mey J. & Gorayska B., *Humane Interfaces: Questions of Methods and Practice in Cognitive Technology*, Amsterdam: North-Holland/Elsevier Science, p. 293-305.

Self, J., draft version 1995, *Computational Mathetics: Towards a Science of Learning Systems Design*, http://cblpc0142.leeds.ac.uk/~jas/cm.html

Self, J., 1990, "Theoretical Foundations for Intelligence Tutoring Systems", AAI/AI-ED Technical Report N° 45, *Journal of Artificial Intelligence in Education*, 1(4), p. 3-14.

Simon, H., & Newell A., 1958, "Heuristic Problem Solving: The Next Advance in Operations Research", *Operations Research 6*, Jan.-Feb.

Tchounikine, P., & Bedbeder M-L., 2003, "Symba: a Tailorable Framework to Support Collective Activities in a Learning Context", *CRIWG 2003, 9th International Workshop on Groupware*, Autrans.

Turkle, S., 1984, *The Second Self, Computers and the Human Spirit*, New York: Simon & Schuster.

Vivet, M., 2000, "Des robots pour apprendre", *Sciences et techniques éducatives*, Vol. 7, n° 1, Paris: Hermès, p. 17-60.

EIGHT SIGNIFICANT EVENTS IN THE 50 YEAR HISTORY OF COMPUTING

T. William Olle
T. William Olle Associates, England
E-mail: BillOlle@aol.com

Abstract: The history of computing is relatively short compared with that of any other area of human knowledge, be it science, engineering, medicine, law, or accounting. On the other hand, the development of the field has been meteoric and computing now occupies a position as a major employer of professional persons, a major facet of industry and a body of knowledge to be disseminated at educational institutions and used - hopefully as a benefit to mankind.

To have a broad perspective on the history of computing for the purposes of education, it is informative to review something like a fifty year period and to identify the really significant events which have paid a major role in developing computing technology as we see it and use it at the present time. This paper is inevitably subjective, but is based on the author's fifty year involvement on different levels and in different facets of computing. The number "eight" is chosen, albeit arbitrarily, as a appropriate number for a subject such as computing.

Key words: Computing; Significant Events; 50 years; Stored program; Ferrite core memory Higher level languages; Disc memory; IBMSystem/360; Data base management; Personal computers; Internet

1. WHAT IS COMPUTING?

The term "computing" is interpreted in this paper as referring to "the use of stored program computers". Some may see this as restrictive in that it does not cover the use of purpose built electromechanical and electronic computers that preceded the development of the stored program electronic computer in 1948. It does not cover the use of accounting machines which some may argue were "programmed" by setting the plug boards. One can even look further back in time and take into account the early use of Hollerith cards that were first used in the 1890s.

2. EDUCATIONAL IMPLICATIONS

Most fields of human knowledge, which have an everyday practical application, have a much longer history than that of computing. When students are taught about such fields, some exposure to the history of the field is almost mandatory. Significant examples are architecture and medicine. It is open to question whether the time spent on this teaching should be one hour or 50 hours. The aim of the teaching of any field should be to put the practical knowledge in the associated course into some kind of temporal context.

3. CRITERIA FOR SIGNIFICANCE

This paper identifies eight events deemed by the author to be significant. The reason for selecting "eight" is that eight is in itself a significant number in the essentially binary world of computing. Four would be too few and sixteen would be too many. Seven was popular in early days, for example when the seven wonders of the ancient world were defined.

The concept of significance is important here. A significant event is regarded basically one which had a major and enduring impact on the practice of computing. It changed the manner in which computers were used and the evidence of the change lasted for a considerable period. An event may possibly have taken time to be assimilated. It may possibly related to two or more similar pieces of work involving different people, taking place in different parts of the world, but collectively over a restricted period.

4. EVENT 1: STORED PROGRAM COMPUTER

Within this framework for significance, the first qualifying event was the first running of a stored program on a general purpose computer. Prior to this event, it had been possible to store data in a computer, but the programs which were to operate on that data were either built-in electro-mechanically or electronically, and defined to the computer using a plug board or by setting dials on the computer.

The first running of a stored program on an (albeit experimental) computer is widely recognized as having taken place at Manchester University in June 1948 [1]. A program was keyed into the computer to evaluate the highest factor of a number. The computer in question used cathode ray tube storage, widely known at the time as Williams tubes after their inventor the late F.C. Williams. The invention of Williams tubes is not in itself seen as a significant event because these were very rapidly superseded by ferrite cores.

The computer was no more than a prototype. To celebrate the 50th anniversary of this event, a working replica was built and is on display in the Manchester Museum of Science and Technology.

In 1949, a "complete" stored program computer known as the EDSAC was taken into use at Cambridge University to provide a computing service to the university.

5. EVENT 2: FERRITE CORES FOR MAIN MEMORY

The arrival of ferrite core storage in the mid 1950s is seen as the second significant event. significant event. This technology was soon widely adapted as fast storage for computers. It was recognized as more economical and more reliable than such alternatives as cathode ray tube storage (William's tubes) and mercury delay lines used in EDSAC.

Some of the earlier work on core memory was carried out at Harvard University in 1949 by An Wang [2], [3]. At nearby MIT, Jay Forrester, working on the Whirlwind project, decided to use ferrite cores rather than William's tubes. The latter were already known to be temperamental and unreliable. An Wang was not granted a patent on ferrite core memory until 1955 by which time it was in use in many places. IBM paid Wang millions of dollars to purchase the patent rights.

The availability and indeed the economics of ferrite cores were helped by the availability of cheap labour in the Far East for assembly. Another advantage of ferrite cores over its rivals was that it could retain its contents indefinitely without power.

Before leaving the subject of ferrite cores, it is important to note that the concept of two levels of storage - one fast, the other less so - is a very early and basic concept which is still totally prevalent today. Ferrite cores have been used for high speed memory, whereas cheaper alternatives such as magnetic tapes and subsequently rotating discs have been used for what used to be called "backing store".

6. EVENT 3: HIGHER LEVEL LANGUAGES

In the early days, programs had to be written using the same set of instructions as the computer itself used, commonly referred to as machine code. There was a gradual evolution from this way of writing programs [4].

The main stepping stone was a symbolic assembler language. This allowed the machines instructions to be replaced in a program by some kind of mnemonic name, such as ADD for an addition and DIV for divide. At the same time the requirement to refer to data by using the machine's own internal addressing system was replaced by a facility for identifying data in a program using more mathematical symbols such as X, Y and Z.

It is important to note that during the 1950s and early 1960s, scientific applications and commercial (or business) applications were treated as very separate indeed. Different kinds of hardware and software were used. As a result of this schism, two separate sets of higher level languages were developed.

One the scientific side, Autocode was developed for the Ferranti Mark 1 at Manchester University by R.A. Brooker and first demonstrated in 1954. Because the Mark 1 had a magnetic drum as its backing store, it was not necessary for an Autocode programmer to bother about transferring data from one level of memory to the other [5].

FORTRAN (an abbreviation for Formula Translation) was developed at IBM between 1954 and 1957 by John W. Backus for the IBM 704 [6]. This machine used magnetic tape drives for backing storage which was a strong reason for including in FORTRAN, the statements for reading and writing data between the core store and a designated tape unit.

ALGOL (Algorithmic Language) was also developed during the 1950s and is the result of dedicated work by many people in many places. An early effort was the Michigan Algorithm Decoder later designated ALGOL 58. There was also an ALGOL 60 and an ALGOL 68 that were the focus for one of the earliest IFIP Working Groups, namely WG2.1 [7].

On the commercial side, there is also a long list of items of early work. One of the earliest is the legendary Grace Hopper's A-O compiler in 1952, followed by ARITH-MATIC (1954), MATH-MATIC and FLOW-MATIC (both 1955). These were all developed while she was at Remington Rand Univac.

The US Department of Defense (DoD) had a major hand in the development of commercial higher level languages. In 1958, DoD was a major force behind the formation of the organization known as CODASYL (Conference on Data Systems Languages). The initial aim of this organization was to specify a Common Business Language, which came to be known as COBOL [8].

One early aim of COBOL was simple. Any accountant should be able to read and write it. In fact, COBOL had a tremendous influence on what was at the time called Business Data Processing.

Higher Level Languages in general have had an enduring impact on computing, but it would be extremely difficult to point to any specific piece of work as the significant event.

7. EVENT 4: IBM SYSTEM/360 RANGE OF COMPUTERS

The fourth event was initiated by an announcement in April 1964 [9]. It lead to the bringing together of computers for scientific applications with computers for business or more broadly speaking administrative applications. It was some time before the first IBM System/360 computers were delivered. At that time IBM had about 85% of the overall market with the remaining 15% shared by seven other manufacturers. Hence, there were frequent references at the time to "IBM and the seven dwarfs."

Prior to this event, many larger corporations were finding it necessary to have both a scientific and a business machine, typically in different departments of the corporation. There could be overlap in peripheral functions such as card punching and printing.

In addition to the hardware, IBM also announced an operating system, namely OS/360 which could handle both kinds of computing. There was knock-on effect on the compilers used to compile previously disparate languages such as FORTRAN and COBOL. Both of these needed to handle input from card readers, output to a printer as well as input and output to magnetic tapes. The systems software previously tailored for the compiler was unified in a part of the operating system called the data management system.

8. EVENT 5: DISCS AS LARGE SCALE MEMORY

The fifth significant event was the development of discs as large scale memory. The assimilation of this technology took quite a long time. The first computer to include a disc drive was introduced by IBM in September 1956

[10]. The computer was the IBM 305 RAMAC and the disc drive was called the "IBM 350 disk drive". It had a capacity of five million 7-bit characters (4.8 megabytes using contemporary jargon).

It is noted in passing that the concept of two levels of storage (also called memory) is one that has been part of computing since the early days and is still to be found in today's personal computers. Early computers used magnetic drums and magnetic tapes. Discs had the advantage over drums that they allowed more data storage in less physical space. They also had the advantage of what was somewhat misleadingly called "random access" based presumably on the IBM RAMAC designation. This terminology soon became more correctly "direct access".

Without examining the economic factors in detail, one can only assume that magnetic tapes survived as long as they did for economic reasons. As larger problems were tackled in both scientific and business computing, there was a need for retaining larger volumes of stored data in computerized form.

However, it was during the 1960s that discs began to find wide spread acceptance. One of the main problems was making effective use of the extra dimension over and above that provided by magnetic tape files and the associated sequential processing.

The Indexed Sequential Access Method (ISAM) soon emerged which made it possible to access a single record in a direct access storage device (typically a disc) other than by scanning through many records as would be necessary with a magnetic tape file. Either an index was maintained, as in ISAM, or else the physical address of the record to be accessed could be calculated from the value of its key item.

9. EVENT 6: DATA BASE MANAGEMENT

The sixth significant event was the evolution of data base technology that itself was enabled by the availability of disc storage. With magnetic tape files it was necessary to scan sequentially through a tape to search for a piece of data. With a database stored on a disc, it became possible to jump from a piece of data in one location on the disc to a piece of data in another location. The early pioneering work on this was started in the early 1960s by Charles Bachman working at General Electric, which at that time was a computer manufacturer. However, the acceptance of this technology took at least a decade and was a major discussion point during the seventies.

Bachman was the first to recognize that discs provided an extra dimension to be exploited when storing and retrieving business records from high volumes of business data. He developed a software system as early as

1963 called Integrated Data Store (IDS) which ran on the General Electric 225[11]. There was clearly a need to process the data stored in the records retrieved. At the time GE was using a language called GECOM as GE version of COBOL had not yet become available.

The future of IDS was strongly influenced by the industry wide acceptance of COBOL as developed by CODASYL. In 1964, US Steel persuaded the CODASYL COBOL Language Committee to investigate the inclusion of the IDS concepts into COBOL. The group charged with this responsibility was initially called the List Processing Task Force but the name was changed in May 1967 to Data Base Task Group (DBTG) [12].

The DBTG specifications were widely implemented around the world by manufacturers of the time but never by the world's dominant manufacturer, namely IBM. IBM adopted its own approach called Information Management System (IMS) in 1967.

In 1970, an IBM employee, the late Edgar H. Codd, published a seminal paper [13] on what came to be recognized as the relational model, not to be confused with the DBTG's network model and IMS's hierarchical model. The seventies proved to be a decade of intense debate over the relative merits of these three models. The debate took place in academia and among practitioners who recognized the importance of making the right decision on how to structure and maintain their employers' all important databases. The relational model is the one which has endured and it is the basis for the ISO SQL standard that all current commercially available database management products claim some kind of conformance.

10. EVENT 7: PERSONAL COMPUTERS

The seventh event also took place over several years [14]. It started as early as 1975 with the availability of kits from which "do it yourself" enthusiasts could build a small personal computer for their own use. There were many significant developments between 1976 and 1981 by companies such as Apple, Commodore, Sinclair and Osborne.

However, it was in August 1981 that IBM introduced the IBM PC. It had a 16 bit CPU (based on an Intel 8088 chip), 16 kilobytes of RAM and two floppy drives. It came with an operating system known as MS-DOS which its implementer, Microsoft, persuaded IBM should not be an IBM exclusive. Ultimately, this had a significant effect on IBM's influence on the burgeoning personal computer industry.

The personal computer brought computing out of the office and research centre into the home and did more than any other event of the eight cited here to increase awareness of computing.

11. EVENT 8: INTERNET

Finally, the eighth event is the development of the Internet [15]. The ability for computers to exchange data across dedicated data links had been possible for some time, but the availability of personal computers, coupled with the dramatic reduction in the cost of telecommunications capacity meant that it was technically possible for two individuals on different sides of the world to communicate with each other by electronic mail.

12. CONCLUSIONS

The selection of what the author considers to be the eight most significant events in the history of computing is inevitably subjective and surely controversial.

It must be emphasized that the sequence in which the events are presented in this paper is "quasi-temporal". One could possibly argue for exchanging the order of events 4 and 5. The omissions of the evolution of operating systems and of silicon chips are felt to be the major omissions.

It is interesting to summarize the breakdown of the eight events listed into hardware, software and both.

Stored program computer hardware and software
Ferrite core memories hardware
Higher level languages software
IBM360 range hardware and software
Discs hardware
Data base management software
Personal computers hardware and software
Internet hardware and software

The term "hardware" with respect to the Internet must include communications hardware.

It is hope that this necessarily brief overview of the history of computing will help stimulate the education of new practitioners into the subject as well as stimulating debate among them.

REFERENCES

Author's note: There are many web references for most of the eight events described in this paper. Those that are cited here represent a modest selection. Each has proved valuable to the author in preparing this paper and are considered to be useful to any student who wishes to dig deeper.

[1] "The Manchester Small Scale Experimental Machine - The Baby" http://www.computer50.org/mark1/new.baby.html
[2] "Magnetic Core Memory - Wikipedia" http://en.wikipedia.org/wiki/Core_memory
[3] "History of Computing Industrial Era 1950 - 1951" http://www.thocp.net/timeline/1950.htm
[4] "Timeline of programming languages - Wikipedia" http://en.wikipedia.org/wiki/Timeline_of_programming_languages
[5] "The significance of Brooker's autocodes in taking early Manchester machines into the market (1954 - 1960)" www.computer50.org/mark1/gethomas/manchester_autocodes.html
[6] "Fortran - Wikipedia " http://en.wikipedia.org/wiki/Fortran
[7] "International Federation for Information Processing Working Group 2.1 ALGOL Bulletin 1959-1976" http://www.cbi.umn.edu/collections/inv/cbi00029.htmlf
[8] "COBOL History - Milestones" http://legacyj.com/cobol/cobol_history.html
[9] "Looking back - April 1964" http://www.beagle-ears.com/lars/engineer/comphist/ibm360.htm
[10] "IBM 305 RAMAC - the first computer with a hard disc drive in 1956" http://www.cedmagic.com/history/ibm-305-ramac.html
[11] "Web project on Charles W. Bachman" http://www.sis.pitt.edu/~mbsclass/hall_of_fame/bachman.htm
[12] "CODASYL: historical background http://www.ee.und.ac.za/coursemain/DNE4DP2/sqlnotes/CODASYL.htm
[13] "A relational model of data for large shared data banks" http://www.acm.orgclassics/nov95/toc.html
[14] "Personal Computer History" http://lowendpc.com/history/index.shtml
[15] Internet Society (ISOC) "All about the Internet: Brief history of the Internet" http://www.isoc.org/internet/history/brief.shtml

TECHNOLOGY LEADING TO HISTORIC CHANGES

The Beginnings of Computer Education in Slovenia

Franci Pivec, Vladislav Rajkovič, and Andrej Jus
SD Informatika, Slovenia
E-mail: franci.pivec@izum.si, vladimir.rajkovic@ijs.si, andrej.jus@infos.si

Abstract: As early as the 1960s, Slovenia, one of the former Yugoslav republics, had already recognized computer science as being the most prospective technology. The World Computer Congress (WCC) held in Ljubljana in 1971, played a very important role in the promotion of computer science. Slovenian school authorities enjoyed relative autonomy in the former Yugoslavia and this made it possible for them to promote computer education. They also had strong support from civil society. This expressed orientation towards an information society was one of the major differences between Slovenia and the rest of the former Yugoslavia and one of the causes contributing to the attainment of Slovenia's independence.

Key words: WCC; Computer education; Computer programming competition, Slovenia

1. INTRODUCTION

The former Yugoslavia [Note 1], a socialist country, was determined to demonstrate its progressiveness, among other things, in science. Consequently, large science and technology centres were built in the capitals of its republics. The centre in Ljubljana, Slovenia, had decided to purchase a Zuse Z-23 computer as early as the end of the 1950s. This was actually the beginning of computing in Slovenia. (The pioneer times of computing in Slovenia are dealt with in a special round table discussion within the Slovenian Informatics Society, web page: www.hist-ri.slo.net.) Computer science was considered to be a field of strategic national importance. The applied mathematics team in Ljubljana was well aware of the significance and attractiveness of the new technology; thus, it offered opportunities to a wide circle of interested young people. After the first IBM and CDC computers had been purchased in the 1960s, the Jožef Stefan Institute (Institut Jožef Stefan) became the first computer education centre in the country. The mission of the Jozef Stefan Institute is the accumulation – and dissemination – of knowledge at the frontiers of natural science and technology to the benefit of society at large through the pursuit of education, learning, research, and development of high technology at the highest international levels of excellence. The Institute is justifiably proud of its achievement of very early introduction of large computing facilities in Slovenia through pooling of resources and the formation of a national computing center.

2. THE IFIP WORLD COMPUTER CONGRESS IN LJUBLJANA

Ljubljana was the only city "on the other side of the Iron Curtain" where the IFIP World Computer Congress was held and that as early as 1971, and those facts had far-reaching consequences. Slovenian computer experts established excellent connections with highly developed environments. As one of the consequences of the IFIP World Computer Congress, the use of computers became the imperative of progress in Slovenian public opinion. At that time, some of the largest computer corporations opened representative offices for the East in Ljubljana (IBM, CDC, Digital, Bourroughs); soon afterwards they also licensed the manufacture of computers (ISKRA, DELTA, GORENJE). The WCC also had a large impact on education. Views on information technology represented one of the major causes for the growing differences between Ljubljana and Belgrade. Based on IT, Slovenia was very much in favour of modern managerial approaches, primarily of the openness to the world, which made a considerable difference in comparison to the governing practices in the former Yugoslavia.

3. THE BEGINNINGS OF COMPUTER EDUCATION

At the end of the 1960s, computer science was introduced in schools in a rather informal way. Young employees of the computer centre at the Jožef Stefan Institute (Bratko, Rajkovič, Lajovic, Hafner, Trampuž, Cokan) offered to conduct optional computer courses in various secondary schools. Such courses, most of them consisting of approximately 40 lessons, usually included elementary computer functions and programming in FORTRAN. These activities received a favourable reaction from the Slovenian Board of Education and, consequently, the Commission for the Introduction of Computer Education into Secondary Schools was established. The Multimedia Centre of the Referral Centre of the University of Zagreb, where, above all, Mužić and Šoljan systematically researched the use of computers in education, had a positive effect on the development in Slovenia.

In 1971, the first seminar for computer science teachers was held. [1] At that time, computer science was taught in a quarter of all Slovenian secondary schools. In 1974, the first Slovenian computer science textbook was published [2]. One year later, when computer science was being taught at a half of all Slovenian schools, the first evaluation was carried out, and the report produced was presented at the IFIP (International Federation of Information Processing) Computers in Education Conference [3]. In 1973, the International Conference on the Use of Computers in Chemical Education was held in Ljubljana. The conference was led by Aleksandra Kornhauser, and it represented the basis for the establishment of the UNESCO International Centre for Chemical Studies (ICCS) [4].

At that time, few schools had their own computers. However, many publicly and privately owned enterprises that had computers offered schools the possibility of terminal and direct access free of charge and with the passionate commitment of computer experts, who were few in number at that time.

The introduction of microcomputers resulted in radical changes in this field. According to Ivan Gerlič [5], this period of time can be divided into two phases:

- the multiform phase (schools purchasing all types of computers available; e.g., Commodore, Apple, BBC, ORIC, Sinclair) and
- the uniform phase (after the decision was made to purchase only IBM-PC compatible computers with uniform MS-DOS operating systems).

In 1983, the first regulation governing hardware and software standardization in schools was issued. Then, computer education was introduced as an optional subject in all primary schools and as a range of compulsory subjects in all grades of secondary schools. In the framework of an all-embracing school reform — which however eventually proved to be rather unsuccessful — a 4-year computer course was introduced in 1981 in one type of secondary schools, and almost 2% of the total school population enrolled. The introduction of a computer science secondary school, probably the first if not the only one of its kind in the world, was a confirmation of the euphoric openness to the new technology and of the great expectations that Slovenian society had for it. Computer secondary schools were in operation for almost a decade; many students who had successfully finished their education there continued their studies at the universities with success and are now among the leading computer experts.

The first computer course was introduced at the University in 1973; electrical engineering and mathematics students could enrol in it after their second year of study. Soon, independent computer departments and, then later, faculties with complete undergraduate and postgraduate programmes developed at the University of Ljubljana as well as at the University of Maribor. It is of special significance that Education Faculties introduced computer education for teachers as early as 1984. The state supported this development trend with a strong information infrastructure (www.arnes.si), which was widely accessible and free of charge, and with a very popular co-operative library system (www.cobiss.si), in which all Slovenian libraries have been participating since the end of the 1980s. To most people, this represents the first practical experience with the advantages of network implementation.

4. THE CIVIL MOVEMENT FOR THE USE OF COMPUTERS

The Association of Organisations for Technical Culture with its widespread network and the goal of popularizing technical innovations, and non-governmental organisations played a large, sometimes even essential, role in the introduction of computer education in Slovenia. In the 1970s, the use of computers became their major focus. They organised computer workshops and exhibitions (such as "Računalnica" and "Računalniški dnevi") which represented a meeting-point for hardware and software providers and users, the latter consisting of teachers and pupils united in their common effort to master the new technology. As a consequence, computer clubs emerged and these were of great assistance to computer education. Nowadays, an exhibition referred to as INFOS (Informatika na Slovenskem, Information Technology in Slovenia) is still active, reminding one of past events in this field [6].

Programming competitions were particularly popular; the first ideas concerning these competitions can be traced back to 1974, earlier than anywhere else in the world, and the first competition was organised in 1977 [7]. Initially, these competitions were targeted towards secondary schools but later also to primary schools including first grade pupils. Without a doubt, Pavel Azalov is wrong when he claims that Bulgarian computer competitions were the first ones of this kind in the world; they were held no earlier than 1982, and, by that time, Slovenia already had a long tradition in the field [8]. The highlight of these competitions was the first International Computer Olympics, held in 1988 in Nova Gorica, Slovenia. Azalov has also ignored this fact and claims that the first Computer Olympics were held in 1989 in the city of Pravec in Bulgaria [9]. Perhaps the misunderstanding has been caused by the name change, as, later on, these competitions were referred to as International Olympiad in Informatics (IOI); however, the Olympics held in Nova Gorica, have been assuredly documented with the publication of its "Problems in Programming" by the Wiley Publishing House [10].

5. CONCLUSION

In the former Yugoslavia, the introduction of ICT (information and communications technology) became a field for the confrontation between different concepts of social development. The field of computer science symbolised an openness to the world, good management practices and ideological neutrality. From this aspect, its significance was similar to "perestroika", "solidarnošč" or "svoboda vyrazu" in other socialist countries. ICT also had an impact on radical changes taking place in the former Yugoslavia. The meteoric rise of computer education in Slovenia led to an historic turn in the country. The idea that the existence of a small nation like Slovenia no longer depended on the "shelter" of some powerful state, but that creative participation in the global network of the information society could also help it survive prevailed. Slovenia, since its independence, has not only been admitted to the EU and NATO, it has also accepted the strategy of the transition into an information society and established the Ministry of Information Society. Excellent examples in this field can be found primarily in the countries of Northern Europe. Those who expressed such a vision as early as the 1960s can only regret that its realization required a long winding path in the modern history of the Balkans; this path, though, would have been rather different for Slovenians without the strong IT connection to the rest of the world.

REFERENCES

[1] Bratko, I., J. Grad, M. Kac, J. Lesjak, J. Virant, E. Zakrajšek (1972) Računalništvo (Gradivo s tečaja za srednješolske profesorje) Ljubljana: Zavod SRS za šolstvo.

[2] Bratko, I., V. Rajkovič (1974) Uvod v računalništvo. Ljubljana: DZS
[3] Bratko, I., V. Rajkovič, B. Roblek (1975) What should secondary school students know about computers: analysis of an experiment. O. Lecarme, R. Lewis (eds) Computer in Education. IFIP, North Holland Publishing, str. 841–846.
[4] Kornhauser, A. (1975) Uporaba računalnika v kemijskem izobraževanju. Vzgoja in izobraževanje, 5. str. 3–24.
[5] Gerlič, I. (2000) Sodobna informacijska tehnologija v izobraževanju. Ljubljana: DZS
[6] Skulj, T. (2003) Ostrenje osti in pršenje na vse strani. Povezave, November, str. 6–7.
[7] Hafner, I. (1977) Prvo republiško tekmovanje iz računalništva. Delo, 21. april, str. 7.
[8] Azalov, P. (1989) Bulgarian Competitions in Informatics, Mathematics Competitions, vol. 2, No. 1, pp. 60–66.
[9] Azalov, P. (1994) IOI '93 – To Mendoza and Back, M&IQ 3/94, vol. 4, pp. 122–131
[10] Vitek, A., I. Tvrdy, K. Reinhart, B. Mohar, M. Martinec, T. Dolenc, V. Batagelj (1991) Problems in programming, Experience through practise, Wiley Professional Computing. Chichester: John Wiley&Sons.

ENDNOTE

1. Slovenia was a part of the former Yugoslavia until 1991. In the former Yugoslavia, the republics (its constituent parts) enjoyed relative autonomy in the areas of the education system, science, culture, health service, etc., whereas the economic and defence systems and foreign policy were centrally governed. Although a sort of convoy strategy was enforced by the federal government, the stage of development achieved and development ambitions of the republics varied to a large extent. Technology successfully evaded ideological control; therefore, attempts for alternative breakthroughs were numerous, especially in more developed areas.

WHAT DID WE THINK WE WERE DOING?

Reflections on the History of Educational Computing in Victoria, Australia

Anthony Jones, Anne McDougall, and John Murnane
The University of Melbourne, Australia
E-mail: A.Jones@unimelb.edu.au; A.Mcdougall@unimelb.edu.au; JMurnane@unimelb.edu.au

Abstract: This paper reflects on some aspects of the introduction of computers into Australian schools and teacher education, with an emphasis on the state of Victoria. Developments in the U.K. and the U.S.A. have significantly influenced Australian educational computing, often being adopted with a local flavor. This is acknowledged here through the use of vignettes that illustrate local incidents, which are then related to occurrences in other Australian states as well as other countries.

Key words: Teacher education; Educational computing; Australia

1. INTRODUCTION

Despite the brief history of educational computing it is impossible to record all the successes, failures and individuals. Herein we consider selected episodes in educational computing in one Australian state, but with links that extend further afield. We claim neither primacy nor uniqueness, knowing of similar occurrences in other places, both earlier and later. We focus through seven vignettes – short descriptive sketches of episodes in which one or other of the authors have participated. It is still possible to talk with some pioneers of educational computing, and such discussions, together with information from archived journals and handbooks, are the major resources for this paper.

2. THE AGE OF ENTHUSIASTS

In the 1970s it might have seemed to some teachers, students and parents that advocates for using the new computing technology in education were curiously obsessed. Computing brought a new language of acronyms and pejorative terms such as "kill", "crash" and "abort", as well as threats to move teaching away from being teacher-centered. Educational administrators faced issues of teacher re-training, supply of hardware and software, and curriculum development, all of which were going to be costly at a time when education was not necessarily a political priority.

Much of what we take for granted today in educational computing can be traced back to the innovative ideas and practices of enthusiasts. The vignettes in this paper occasionally identify enthusiasts, but always acknowledge their conviction and efforts.

Vignette 1: Computing in teacher education, 1970.

In March 1970 students majoring in mathematics at Bendigo Teachers' College are busily translating simple mathematical formulae into the only high level programming language available to them, FORTRAN IV, and transcribing the code line by line onto coding sheets.

A week later students receive cards wrapped in computer printout. The lecturer had taken their coding sheets to the computing facility at the local higher education institution, and then returned several days later to collect the processed output. As students read their printout there are moans, exclamations and occasional sounds of triumph. Following a quick check of individual success or failure the students begin trying to understand the error messages in their printout. If there are many errors the whole program is again transcribed onto coding sheets, ready to be re-punched and batch processed.

The following year the students commence their career as classroom teachers. All are assigned to rural primary schools without access to computers.

Prior to 1970 very few Australian teacher education students had any contact with computers. While universities had computers and taught computer science, school computing activities were almost non-existent. Then teacher education institutions began to recruit mathematics and science staff with some computing background. Around this time the authors of this paper were appointed to teacher education positions but did not have computing in their job description. Because of the growing interest in computing in schools, all three were soon involved in teaching computing and supervising research in the area.

Prior to desktop computers becoming readily available, few teachers had access to the mainframe or minicomputers used in higher education, severely restricting the scope and content of hardware related topics; there was a strong emphasis on teaching programming, with a mathematical bias.

Vignette 2: Formal computing qualifications for teachers.

By 1975 formal computer education for Victorian teachers was provided through post-graduate B.Ed. degrees offered by most faculties of education. In Melbourne undergraduate pre-service primary and secondary teacher education courses were offered at the Melbourne College of Advanced Education (MCAE), while post-graduate courses were available at the University of Melbourne..

The 1975 pre-service educational computing subjects were incorporated into mathematics. For secondary teachers MCAE offered elective subjects at different levels of the four-year course. "Computer Programming" (FORTRAN IV); "Computer Science I" containing searching and sorting algorithms, assembly language, Boolean algebra, and data structures; and "Computer Science II" covering the history of computing, simulations, Turing machines, data structures, operating systems, social implications, and computers in education.

The University of Melbourne offered only two postgraduate subjects: an introduction to programming, and an investigation of educational uses of computers.

According to Walker (1991) the first Australian school microcomputer project began in 1976 when two teachers from a Melbourne non-government school turned their personal interest in microcomputers into an exploration of the educational potential of this technology.

Vignette 3: Government funding for a school computing project.

Subsequently the two teachers applied for and received a Commonwealth Schools Commission Innovation Program grant to develop their interest in microcomputers into an educational initiative in the school in which they both worked. They were required to locate hardware suitable for use in the school. Secondly, they were to produce software, practically all of which had, in the beginning, to be written personally. Finally, they were required to publish a newsletter to promulgate their activities. (Walker, 1991, p.296)

In an era of "plug and play" hardware and self-installing software, it is difficult to imagine the challenges faced by these two teachers. By 1980 computer hardware and software were progressing in directions unimagined by engineers and researchers in the 1950s and 1960s. Paradoxically, hardware size and cost decreased while operating speed, memory size and versatility of application increased. Until the late 1970s almost all computer use was based around mainframe computers or minicomputers. Although large, slow and inflexible by today's standards, the Digital Equipment Corporation PDP family of minicomputers made educational uses feasible. Compared with other computers of the time, the PDP-8 was an inexpensive general purpose computer suitable for use in a variety of roles in higher education.

Australian researchers were following with interest developments in educational computing taking place in the USA and the UK. Bitzer and others at the University of Illinois had developed the PLATO project, breaking new ground both conceptually and technologically. Based on mainframe hardware, PLATO introduced educators to time-sharing, computer games, and what became e-mail and newsgroups. Using acoustic couplers and the telephone system, workstations were able to operate well away from the Illinois campus – even as far away as Australia.

Early research into computer assisted instruction by Patrick Suppes and Richard Atkinson at Stanford University had investigated using computers to teach the basics of reading and mathematics. The program for learning mathematics was highly structured, was based on behaviorist learning principles, and included programmed feedback to learners, lesson branching, and record keeping for student attainment and progress.

Overseas journals including *Technical Horizons in Education* (1972), *Creative Computing* (1974), the *Oregon Computing Teacher* (1974), (subsequently *The Computing Teacher* (1979) then *Leading and Learning with Technology* (1995)) were avidly read by Australian computer education enthusiasts. The first educational computing journal produced in Australia arose from the research grant outlined in Vignette 3. *COM-3* began in 1977, was edited by Tim Mowchanuk and published at Essendon Grammar School where he taught. In early issues it was stated that, *COM-3 stands for the first three letters of the words, COMMUNITY COMPUTER COMMUNICATION. It stands for all permutations and combinations of these words and symbolizes the role of the computer in altering our society through its powerful information processing capabilities.* (Mowchanuk, 1977, p.1) *COM-3* became the official journal of the Computer Education Group of Victoria (CEGV), reaching educational computing enthusiasts throughout Australia.

Vignette 4: Enthusiastic educators form a professional association.

In May 1978 a public meeting led to the formation of the Computer Education Group of Victoria. Initially supported by a mathematics teacher association, the CEGV organized and ran a national educational computing conference in 1979 and by linking up with the two teachers noted in Vignette 3 began to produce a journal on a regular basis.

Although a state-based association, the first CEGV conference featured keynote speakers from education systems, schools, and universities from several Australian states. CEGV conferences have become annual events, even though there is now a national educational computing association with a bi-annual national conference. The first US National Educational Computing Conference (NECC) was held in 1979. An Australian national association was formed in 1982, a national conference held in 1983, and the first issue of a national journal, *Australian Educational Computing*, was published in July 1986.

The first CEGV conference enabled early users of computers in education to meet with fellow enthusiasts, and to realize they were not alone, a point reinforced by the attendance of interstate teachers and a display of hardware, software and publications from around the world. The emphasis has always been on computer applications and their relevance to teaching and learning in Australian classrooms, although some research is reported. In 1979 many conference sessions demonstrated software developed by teachers, including programs for displaying Chinese characters, teaching German, drill in mathematics and English, and a student records and school accounting system.

Seymour Papert was the major drawing card for more than 1000 participants at the third CEGV conference in 1981. Scott Brownell from the Elizabeth Computing Centre in Tasmania had introduced LOGO into Australia in 1975 following a visit to the Artificial Intelligence Laboratory at MIT. Originally running on a DEC minicomputer situated in Hobart, Tasmania, access and use were limited because equipment had to be transported to a school, and connected to the phone network via an acoustic coupler. Sandra Wills, who was almost synonymous with LOGO in Australia in the period 1976-82, moved equipment around the state and demonstrated the potential of LOGO. Within a few years Tasmanian schools accessed LOGO via teletypes and terminals connected to the statewide time-share network. In Victoria and other states without networks, teletypes linked to the telephone system via acoustic couplers enabled some students to experience LOGO.

By the early 1980s several Australian authors had published books proposing innovative approaches to learning through LOGO. *Learning LOGO on the Apple II* (McDougall, Adams & Adams, 1982) gained a worldwide audience as the authors adapted the content to reflect different dialects of LOGO running on computers such as the BBC micro, Commodore-64, and Tandy TRS-80. The book was translated into French, German and Chinese. Also locally authored in the same period, *Let's Talk Apple Turtle* (Nevile & Dowling, 1983) was aimed at younger children and linked LOGO to off-computer activities including writing stories, drawing, and making models.

Vignette 5: A personal computer in a primary classroom.

In the grade 6 classroom of a small independent primary school in Bendigo, the teacher, his class, a group of teacher education students, and a teacher educator are all gathered around a small VIC-20 computer. It is 1982 and the VIC-20 has recently become available in Australia but is still a rarity in schools.

Programming in BASIC the teacher and teacher educator developed a series of simple educational programs for students to use. Many of these programs involved students recalling factual knowledge, and were variations of the drill and practice format.

This was not the first such occurrence, even in Australia, and is included because it illustrates one of the most significant milestones in educational computing. 4- and then 8-bit microprocessors were released in the 1970s, followed by the first personal or desktop computers. Microcomputers bearing brand names including Apple, Atari, Commodore, and Tandy were available in Australia in the early 1980s, and soon appeared in schools and teacher education institutions.

3. MOVING TO FORMALIZATION

As schools and teacher education institutions investigated teaching and learning applications of microcomputers in the late 1970s, one Australian state took a different path. Partly due to geographic features – an island with relatively small land area and with almost all the population living in a few urban centers – Tasmania opted for time-shared networking based on minicomputers.

> *The computer network has been established over the past six years to provide the hardware for computing subjects and computer-based school administration in High schools, Matriculation colleges and Technical colleges.*
>
> *Computing access is currently made available using a network of five PDP-8 computers which act as terminal concentrators to the central PDP-11/70. This system allows schools anywhere in the state, to connect on-line terminals to their nearest PDP-8 node. Nodes are located at Devonport, Burnie, Launceston and Hobart.*
>
> (Brownell, 1977, p.31)

McDougall (1980) made no specific recommendations for hardware, although she acknowledged the imminent spread of microcomputers. In our era of constant hardware and software change it is worth noting the following comment, *It is recommended that, <u>once adequately prepared teachers are available</u>, each school own a micro-computer or interactive terminal facility* (McDougall, 1980, p,32) (emphasis added). This value placed on professional development was reflected in subsequent government policies and actions. State and federal funding in Victoria were channeled into teacher education and support, with successive governments showing little inclination to fund hardware for schools.

With computers becoming commonplace in educational institutions, administrators saw a need to develop formal computing curricula. In Victoria this process began with a subject at Year 12, the final year of secondary schooling. A description of the proposed subject noted that a similar subject *has been available to HSC students in Tasmania for the last 3 years, has been generally available in the U.K. for around 4 years and in the U.S.A. for at least 6 years* (Montgomery, 1978, p.19). The proposed Computer Science subject consisted of four (unequal) parts: software; hardware; applications; social implications. The plan was for a core (computer structure, algorithms, programming, data structures, file manipulation), which comprised two-thirds of the total teaching time, and two options from social implications, system case studies, and installation inspections. Then, as now, practical work was to form a significant part of the subject. By the time the subject was taught there were local textbooks available, with Woodhouse, Johnstone and McDougall (1982) and Montgomery and Juliff (1981) being popular.

With the introduction of the Year 12 Computer Science subject it became necessary to prepare teachers for this new discipline. Most Australian secondary teachers acquire an undergraduate degree with appropriate subject combinations, and then undertake a one-year Graduate Diploma in

Education. In 1981 the University of Melbourne included computer science as a teaching method in the Graduate Diploma in Education (Secondary). Although the focus was on content and assessment related to the new Year 12 subject, teaching computing at lower secondary levels was also covered. Woodhouse and McDougall (1986) is an example of an early computing textbook written specifically for teachers in training.

Vignette 6: University research and development, 1973.

In 1973 three students of first year Swedish are huddled around one of two interactive terminals located near the entrance of the University of Melbourne's Computer Centre. They read books balanced on their knees, filling in time while waiting for the computer to respond to their last typed message.

The Swedish vocabulary drill program they are using is the first software developed by the recently established Computers in Education Research Group. Despite the slow response time of the (primarily batch processing) computer, special letter combinations used to replace the accents normally used in Swedish, and the need to type instead of hand-write responses, student evaluation of the program is (astonishingly to us now) very positive.

Although early computers were inappropriate for the task, serious thinking about computer support for learning had begun in the University, and valuable experience was gained in educational software design. The Group developed programs to support teaching in a range of disciplines. Technical reports were produced describing the development and evaluation of the programs, and the experience gained contributed to development of an elective course, Educational Uses of Computers, for postgraduate education students in 1974.

Acceptance of both IT skills and classroom applications of IT as core pre-service teacher education for all new teachers in Victoria occurred some years after various aspects of IT became part of the primary and secondary school curriculum. Because many pre-service teacher education institutions believed that IT had educational implications for all teachers, and they were aware of developments in teaching with and about IT in local and overseas schools, there is a long history of IT in Victorian teacher education. IT subjects for teachers in training began in the early 1970s. Initially they were offered only as parts of other discipline areas, most often mathematics. In 1984 Monash University introduced a mandatory IT in education subject as part of the Graduate Diploma in Education (Secondary) course. This appears to be the first Australian mandatory IT specific course for prospective teachers, occurring well before the Victorian Government notified teacher education institutions in 1997 that it would soon employ only graduating teachers who had successfully completed a subject that ensured competence in basic IT skills, knowledge, and classroom applications.

Throughout the 1960s, 1970s and 1980s much educational computing in Australia was piecemeal and reliant on the skills and knowledge of an ever-increasing band of enthusiasts. Even when education systems began to formalize school computing curricula and teacher credentialing, progress was gradual and often inconsistent between various authorities.

4. NOW AND TOMORROW

Finally, we take a brief look at some current developments in educational computing and then a glance toward the future. Society in 2004 is technologically rich and is becoming technology dependent in many aspects of life. Microprocessors are ubiquitous and now monitor, control and enable us to do things that were not even dreams half a century ago. Teachers are provided with notebook computers to support their professionalism (McDougall, Nicholson & Marshal, 2000), and are now under increasing pressure to use computer technology effectively, efficiently and often.

Vignette 7: Computing in teacher education, 2003.

As part of initial teacher education for primary teachers at the University of Melbourne, a Problem Based Learning (PBL) approach to learning in a technology rich environment has been implemented. Students are presented with four problems that they solve in collaborative groups. The context for all problems is a "virtual" primary school that students access through a website. From this site students can find school policy and curriculum documents as well as individual profiles of all staff members and information about class sizes and the physical aspects of the school campus.

The room in which classes are held for this subject has ten oval-shaped tables. Each table has a computer monitor set into the top, with the rest of the computer on shelves underneath. The computers are standard university machines with internet and intranet connections, as well as the facility to connect to a ceiling-mounted video projector. The tables are sufficiently large to enable five students to sit around one side and view the computer monitor.

The most significant differences between events described in Vignettes 1 and 7 are not concerned with advances in technology, but rather with the role of the technology. In Vignette 1 technology is central to the activity; the activity would be senseless without computers, even though computers were not physically accessible by the users. In Vignette 7 the technology has become a means to an end and is no longer the focus of the activity, even though it is more powerful, more sophisticated and more readily available. We are confident this trend will continue as educators learn more about the interconnections between teaching, learning and technology.

5. REFERENCES

Brownell, S., 1977, Elizabeth Computer Centre expands its facilities. *COM-3.* **4**:19.

McDougall, A., 1980, *Computers and post-primary education in Victoria*, Computer Policy Committee, Victorian Education Department: Melbourne.

McDougall, A., Adams, T., and Adams, P., 1982, *Learning LOGO on the Apple II*, Prentice-Hall: Sydney.

McDougall, A., Nicholson, P., and Marshall, A., 2000, Notebook computers for teachers and principals: An initiative of the Department of Education, Employment and Training in Victoria, Australia, in *Proceedings of Conference on Educational Uses of Information and Communication Technologies*, D. Benzie and D. Passey, eds., Beijing, China, pp. 298-301.

Montgomery, A., 1978, HSC Computer Science, *COM-3.* **11**: 19-36.

Montgomery, A. and Juliff, P., 1981, *Introduction to Computer Science*, Prentice-Hall: Sydney.

Mowchanuk, T. (1977). *COM-3.* **4**:1.

Nevile, L., and Dowling, C., 1983, *Let's Talk Apple turtle*, Prentice-Hall: Sydney.

Walker, R., 1991, The development of educational computing policy in the Victorian school system, 1976-1985, *Australian Journal of Education,* **35**(3):292-313.

Woodhouse, D., Johnstone, G., and McDougall, A., 1982, *Computer Science*, John Wiley & Sons: Brisbane.

Woodhouse, D., and McDougall, A., 1982, *Computers: Promise and Challenge in Education*, Blackwell Scientific: Melbourne.

ICT IN CATALAN SCHOOLS

A Look at its Foundations and Early Developments

Jordi Castells i Prims and Ferran Ruiz i Tarragó
Generalitat de Catalunya, Spain
E-mail: jcastell@pie.xtec.es; ferran@pie.xtec.es

Abstract: The authors of this article have been – and continue to be – in charge of the Catalan project of educational integration of ICT since 1986, when the Department of Education of the Generalitat set up its Educational Computing Programme (Programa d'Informàtica Educativa - PIE) with the objective of boosting computing in Catalan schools, within a framework of political decentralization and educational reform. This article aims to look at the initial period of its endeavour –the decade that goes from 1986 to 1995, from the start of the PIE until the appearance of Internet– with the aim of revising, with the perspective of the years gone by, the intentions and results of decisions taken, and, at the same time its influence in the birth and evolution of an organisational model of educational integration of ICT in Catalonia.

Key words: Primary schools; Secondary schools; Teacher training; Curricular integration; Educational telecommunications; Information technology integration policy

1. INTRODUCTION

Catalonia is an historic community within the Spanish state, with a population of more than 6.5 million inhabitants, 3,800 schools and 82,000 teachers serving more that one million students. Approximately 63% of these schools are state-owned, and the rest are privately-owned - although a substantial number are subsidised - where a large part of the running costs of the school are financed with public funds. The Department of Education of the Catalan Government is politically and administratively responsible for the management of education in Catalonia.

In 1986 the Government of Catalonia set up an specific unit within the Department of Education, the Educational Computing Programme

(Programa d'Informàtica Educativa - PIE), with the aim of promoting educational innovation by the use of computing in schools.

The setting up of PIE, together with other action programmes, took place at a time when the educational system found itself immersed in a process of infrastructure change and strong growth, as well as change and reform of the syllabii and associated curricular models. This process also implied the boosting of a new curricular model, which gave prevalence, among other concepts, to active and interdisciplinary action, and gave rise to considerable organisational changes in the system, such as extending the age of compulsory education from 14 to 16 years and the reformulation of secondary education and professional training.

2. OBJECTIVES

The general objective of promoting the use of computers in education in an integrated way was stated within the framework of the following premises:

- Computing was seen as a powerful instrument to favour and encourage positive changes in students' learning and in teaching methods and contents.
- The projects were to encourage the maximum participation possible by all those involved in the educational system.
- Computing was seen as a powerful and versatile instrument that offered a variety of possible approaches, each one of them with its specific advantages and contributions. The PIE addressed this variety, establishing priorities among the different ways of possible use, according to the amount of available hardware and circumstances of each specific project and surroundings.

So as to be able to carry out its work in a suitable way, the educational Administration assumed responsibility for the different aspects related to the introduction of computing in the educational system:

- Acquisition and distribution of materials (hardware and software).
- Teacher training and support.
- Curricular development activities with the help of Information Technology.
- Development and support of communication, information and documentation resources.

Each of these aspects gave rise to a number of actions which will be described and assessed hereunder.

3. ACQUISITION AND DISTRIBUTION OF MATERIALS

During the period under study, between 1986 and 1995, computers were distributed to a total of 1,250 state schools and 200 support centres or educational services, covering all secondary and vocational schools and 50% of state primary schools. From the start there was a commitment towards extensive action, which referred to a large number of schools. So the first action, from 1986-1989, already included all secondary education schools, with a total of 3,500 computers distributed among the 500 secondary education schools, and a smaller number of primary education schools, which was progressively increased in the following years, supplying all schools in Catalonia by 1996, which already lies beyond the time span of this paper.

The hardware supplied to schools was primarily standard market products. Particularly the standard PC was adopted (with the exception of a few Unix workstations for vocational training), due to the wide range of suppliers of existing hardware and software. The educational specificities appeared in the form of peripherals (concept keyboards for very young learners, Computer Assisted Experimentation sensors for assignments in scientific subjects, etc.) and other hardware accessories. The hardware that was distributed at all times included features of state-of-the-art technology, such as hard disk drives and colour monitors. We underline the fact that from 1988 all equipped schools had a modem at their disposal to access telecommunications services, and a separate connection for the computer hooked up to the local network. This was boosted in the 1990/1991 academic year with the installation of local area networks in vocational schools; or with multi-media computers in 1991.

The basic platform was the operating system MS-DOS and later MS Windows. Once consolidated, Windows has been used most widely in the Catalan educational system, and has only been countered with the maturing of free software, again not within the time-span of this survey.

It is worth underlining that there was, and continues to be, a widespread use of "professional" programmes not specifically intended for education: wordprocessors, databases, spreadsheets, artistic and technical drawing programmes, statistical packages, etc., in keeping with the paradigm of using the computer as an instrument of intellectual work. Thus, during the first years, the intensive use of the integrated package Framework was particularly relevant, This program was later replaced by Office, the integrated package from Microsoft. Together with the "professional" programmes, "educational" programmes were used with specific approaches and objectives. Initially the degree of use was low due to the fact that these products were less available, and the difficulty of adapting products coming from other environments, but the degree of their use increased progressively. PIE lent support in the acquisition or production of such programmes. This then gave rise to locally produced products, such as the text editor for children Quadern, the related environment Electra; the open environment supporting activities CLIC; musical editor and interpreter MUSIC; Computer Assisted Experimentation environment; geographic work environment WINGEO; etc. On the other hand, products from external companies and entities were acquired and used, among which we should like to point out the geometric laboratory CABRI, the working environment WINLOGO, the electronic laboratory Electronics Workbench, and the set of educational applications associated with the touch-sensitive keyboard DIL. During the last years of that period there was a proliferation of multi-media programmes especially relevant in enriching teaching methods in a large variety of learning areas and styles.

Some of the developments of that time have left a consolidated seed, both as new products and in effective working methodologies: CLIC, developed by Francesc Busquets, has had a highly relevant success, with over 100,000 educational activities developed by teachers worldwide, which has led to a recent reprogramming that allows those educational activities to be accessed from the Internet.

Some locally produced programmes have been substituted or added to by professional programmes that covered the same area of activity: MUSIC, also developed by Francesc Busquets, has been substituted by Music Time; the EXAO locally produced programmes have been upgraded for use in high-schools science classrooms which include specialised peripherals and software, such as microscopes or consoles that control sets of specialised sensors.

LOGO enjoyed a considerable level of interest but its use was already dropping by mid-nineties. One possible cause is that the dramatic increase of learning opportunities provided by standard and educational software meant a decreasing emphasis on programming as a learning tool.

It is worth pointing out that almost all programmes, both professional and educational, are in Catalan language or have versions in it. In many cases specific translations and adaptations were made.

4. TEACHER TRAINING AND SUPPORT

Right from the start it was thought that the effect on a large sector of teachers was an important requirement for the success of an educational integration policy in computing. Thus, the teacher training action was especially intense. Throughout the analysed period, over 28,000 teachers did courses in different areas of educational computing. Most of the training consisted of modules averaging 30 to 60 hours in length that were attended throughout the Catalan territory by working teachers who combined training with their normal work, using an organizational model previously developed in the "Applied Computing Cycle" at the Polytechnical University of Catalonia.

A significant exception has to be pointed out: before setting up the PIE and for the first years of its existence, some "intensive" courses lasting one year were held. Those courses were attended by teachers who were released from their usual work for a whole academic year. This strategy resulted in a good number of teacher trainers, very well qualified in educational computing. They, in turn, where the leaders of the snowball process of teacher training.

Telematic in-service training of teachers began quite early, in 1989 (Ruiz, 90). From the beginning it became clear that such courses provide high levels of time-space flexibility, very much appreciated by teachers, although telecommunication facilities were somewhat fragile and costs were high.

The training methods used throughout this period have mostly been consolidated, giving rise to a wide offer of in-service training for teachers. Currently almost 25,000 teachers take part every year in training activities for teachers on information technologies and their educational uses. From the start, in conjunction with the training, there existed infrastructures lending support to teachers in their daily work in computing, giving rise both to the provision of training, information, and work materials as well as promoting communication among teachers so as to provide an exchange of experience and information.

The most relevant instruments to achieve this were the support services provided by external firms and the Up-dating Seminars on Information Technologies, known as SATI (Catalan acronym).

Service companies have been very important in providing on-going support, maintenance and professional advice. During the first stage these actions were centered on providing technical maintenance and support to hardware, as well as logic maintenance (audits, consultancy and assessment services) in complex issues such as local area network environments or Unix workstations. In recent years, the proliferation of computer hardware, its increased complexity, the new infrastructures of connectivity and access to the Internet have increased significantly the need of hardware maintenance and of external support. This has have become a vital condition for achieving success with information technology in the school.

The SATI have been – and continue to be – a key part in boosting the successful use of computing in schools. Set up during the first years of PIE, they consist of decentralised meetings throughout the Catalan territory, which are held simultaneously 3 to 7 times per academic year. The Department of Education calls and co-ordinates these meetings, with the list of topics to be dealt with, and prepares the general information and materials to be handed out at the meetings, and also collects highly significant information and opinions with regard to running and assessing the global work project. The seminars in themselves are an important exchange of experiences among participating teachers, contributing to spreading and consolidating successful ways of educational integration of computing.

5. CURRICULAR DEVELOPMENT ACTIVITIES

Curricular development activities through Information Technology are the end objective towards which the actions in this area converge. The real use of hardware and computer programmes was in the daily teaching work, with the objective of integrating these into educational practice.

As has already been mentioned, from the very start, the versatility of the computing instrument favoured a variety of possible uses in education, under different forms or models of action. From the outset, one of the most widespread models in schools in Catalonia was the idea of the computer as an instrument of intellectual work to be integrated into the normal learning work of pupils, to encourage the development of their capacities. The availability of the computing instrument, together with the professional programmes that go with it, very often enables the carrying out of projects or activities that would not be possible without it. Examples of concrete lines of development in this area of action were: work with standard office computer system tools (word processors, databases and spreadsheets, desktop publishing programmes), artistic and technical design and drawing, the use of computing in musical education, robotics, Computer Assisted Experimentation, the use of statistics packages, meteorology and collaborative work using telematics.

On the whole, the use of computing was intended to carry out tasks in different areas and contexts, in a similar way to which this occurs in different facets of society. It may be stressed that the studies were – and continue to be – more interdisciplinary and global in primary education than in secondary education, where the in-depth study in different specific areas or subjects becomes more important. The work carried out in vocational training warrants special mention. In a considerable number of schools this had specialised classrooms in different areas (office computer systems, industrial, hotel management, fashion and the clothing industry) consisting of a series of computers connected via a local network. Initially these used

Novell Netware operating system and later Microsoft environments, equipped with a series of relevant software for the area in question.

Another area of action of considerable importance was the setting up of "Computing Labs", made up of a series of multimedia computers connected via a network of Windows operating system. This lent support to work carried out in different curricular areas, with special attention to language learning, where the ease of having at one's disposal multimedia materials and access to communications are worth stressing. The provision of these laboratories has been fully consolidated, and these have now become "Multimedia Labs" without being linked to any specific area of use, since computing has proven to be valuable as an aid in all curricular areas.

In addition to the model and projects already mentioned, there co-existed a variety of alternative working methods. Thus, the teaching of computing as a specific subject of study was carried out in a large number of schools, often as a conceptual and reference framework that included the presentation of the areas of end-user application that are most widely consolidated today, but also that support a specific programming or developmental technology. Another noteworthy reference was that of the work with LOGO, in projects and activities encouraging the development of students' cognitive capacities, though the intensity of its use has diminished over the past few years. The use of educational programmes in specific areas also took place, especially favoured by the arrival of powerful and easy-to-use multimedia programmes, as well as the support given to areas of specific use. These included work in the school library, where the PERGAM programme is used, developed in PIE, or the more generic use of documentary databases as an instrument of conceptual collection and organization of information in diverse curricular areas.

6. COMMUNICATION, INFORMATION AND DOCUMENTATION RESOURCES

The training, support and backing structures mentioned in the above sections were supplemented with the development of two major projects in the area of communication, information and documentation: The Catalan educational telecommunications network XTEC and the educational resources database SINERA.

Since the PIE began its operations telematics were a very important issue to foster and implement, so in 1988 the Catalan Educational Telecommunications Network was created (XTEC; Xarxa Telemàtica Educativa de Catalunya). During the first stage, XTEC was implemented according to videotex protocol, which at that time was the incipient communication standard in Spain, following the model adopted in other countries, especially in France. The videotex was a limited yet effective system of communication and access to information, although its was clearly limited for other activities such as tele-debates or exchange of materials linked to collaborative work processes. To overcome those limitations some services were developed under a private full-duplex communication protocol that was not subject to the technical drawbacks of the videotex.

XTEC enabled carrying out a considerable number of collaborative working activities among schools according to different formats and strategies. Among these were the secondary school tele-debates in different curricular areas, such as language and literature, and ethics and social sciences. XTEC also allowed the development of international communication activities, with noteworthy contributions in foreign language learning, and gave support to the work of specific groups of people, such as the Pedagogical Resources Centres, the teachers and students of rural schools, or the groupwork activities carried out by teachers of primary education (Ruiz, 1992; Castells, 1993).

The XTEC network was integrated into the Internet in April 1995, and the Department of Education became a supplier of Internet services for Catalan schools. The adoption of Internet has meant a considerable increase in the use of XTEC as a powerful tool specific for the education sector, having considerable impact in almost every area of educational use of ICT. Many of the educational work models that have been mentioned in this article have been boosted and amplified by Internet, and it has made new ones possible as well. The capacity of the Internet to become a global "médiathèque" and its far-reaching communication facilities improved the working standards of XTEC from the start. The information resources and the community dimension of the XTEC and the face-to-face interaction provided by the web of seminars were crucial for teachers becoming acquainted with the materials available in many curricular areas (Vergés, 1994; Castells, 1995a; Castells, 1995b). The continuing success of XTEC as a solid educational reference enabled the creation in 2001 of a specific portal for students, edu365.com, but this lies clearly outside the time-span of this article.

The work done on document databases and specifically on the SINERA (System of Educational Information and Resources for Learning) database, was shown to be a key resource and a quality factor backing the task developed by the PIE in the early years of its operation. The SINERA database (Canet, 1994) was implemented according to the models of professional document databases - distinct of the more classical bibliographical approaches - and contained many thousands of references to educational resources, which were provided by a network of suppliers, both teachers and specialists on educational materials. These were described in accordance with a design that stressed the educational value of every resource. This was achieved by giving each field of the database register a general meaning that was then implemented according to the specificity of the resource.

SINERA was initially implemented on the Mistral document database management system, and was accessible both in the videotex and full-duplex protocols of the XTEC. Later, with the coming-of-age of multimedia standards, it was distributed in CD-ROM, a media that offered greater information storage and distribution capacities. When in later years, with the appearance of Internet, there was an explosion in the magnitude of educational resources stored in digital format, it was no longer possible to continue the development of SINERA. Its methodology has nevertheless survived as the indexing method of the "médiathèques" of the Pedagogical Resources Centres of the Department of Education.

The availability of a truly efficient cataloguing and retrieving system for the educational resources available on the XTEC, including the edu365.com portal, is a pending issue. Even though the available searchers on the Internet (Yahoo, Google, etc) help to gain access to available resources, they were not specifically intended to address the needs of students who are looking for the resources to satisfy a learning need, quite often ill-defined. To fulfill this gap it is being considered to take up the experience of SINERA, coupling it with the new description standards and the technical possibilities that are offered by systems of advanced linguistic analysis, so a balanced model of indexing and retrieving of educational resources suited to the new situation can be put in place.

7. CONCLUSIONS

This article has mentioned a series of actions organised in a simultaneous and coherent fashion by the Educational Computing Programme of the Government of Catalonia in order to introduce computers and promote its educational use in the schools.

New learning opportunities and teaching models, new forms of classroom organization and school work brought about by momentous technological changes are continuously emerging and being explored. The appearance of the local area network fostered the use of computer laboratories, multimedia computers provided access to an entirely new brands of interactive educational contents, and the appearance of the Internet consolidated the social use of telecommunications and boosted the communication and collaboration aspects of learning and school work.

The existence of a coherent organizational and support model has proven to be a key factor for helping schools and teachers on the hard task of integrating information technology into education. The authors of this paper believe that such an integrated policy is still valid at the time of writing this article and that it will become even more critical in the near future, in which the gap between new cohorts of students living immersed in technology since their childhood and a school system that operates on industrial age paradigms will most probably widen (Ruiz, 2003).

REFERENCES

Canet, J., 1994, Document Database Technology in Education in Catalunya, *Telematics in Education. The European Case*, W. Veen et al. ed. Academic Book Centre, ABC, De Lier, The Netherlands, 1994.

Castells, J., 1992, Telematic services in Catalan schools: Working environment and achievements, *IFIP Transactions. Education and Society. Information Processing 92*. Vol 2. R.M. Aiken, ed.

Castells, J., 1993, *Patterns of activity, working conditions and tools in the use of telecommunications in catalan schools*. Lecture given at the conference "Tele Teaching 93", Trondheim, August 1993.

Castells, J., 1995a, XTEC - Xarxa Telemàtica Educativa de Catalunya, *Crònica d'Ensenyament*, May 1995.

Castells, J., 1995b, Experiències en la utilització educativa de la telemàtica, *Crònica d'Ensenyament*, May 1995.

Ruiz, F., Vivancos, J., Baldrich, J., 1990, XTEC Online In service Teacher Training Project, *Learning Technology in the European Communities*. Proceedings of the Delta Conference on Research and Development, The Hague 18-19 October 1990, Kluwer Academic Publishers.

Ruiz, F., 1992, Educational Telecommunications Services: A case study on an integrated approach, *IFIP Transactions. Education and Society*, Information Processing 92. Vol 2. RM Aiken, ed.

Ruiz, F., 1993, *Integration of Information Technology into Secundary Education. Main Issues and Perspectives*, IFIP Working Group 3.1. Guidelines for Good Practice, Vol. 2, Geneva, IFIP Secretariat.

Ruiz, F., 2003, Lecture given at the conference "Education and IT: The Next Ten Years", Barcelona, 8-10 October 2003, http://www.cisco.com/global/ES/events/presencial/educationit/edu_home.shtml

Vergés, M., 1994, Experience in the use of telecommunications in Catalan Schools, *Telematics in Education. The European Case,*. W. Veen et al. ed, Academic Book Centre, ABC, De Lier, The Netherlands, 1994.

STREAMS IN THE HISTORY OF COMPUTER EDUCATION IN AUSTRALIA

An Overview of School and University Computer Education

Arthur Tatnall and Bill Davey
Victoria University and RMIT University Australia
E-mail: arthur.tatnall@vu.edu.au

Abstract: In world terms, Australia moved into the educational computing, both at the Higher Education and School levels, very early. This paper looks at how university subjects, and later how whole courses in computing evolved in Australia and how these had very little effect on the later use of computers in schools. We briefly examine how computers were first used in schools, and the influences that put them there and decided how they could be used. We relate an established a model of the growth of academic subjects to the emergence of the discipline area of computing, and in particular, to the Victorian Year 12 Computer Science subject.

Key words: Computer science; Information systems; Computer education; Computers across the curriculum; School computing; University computing.

1. INTRODUCTION

The Commonwealth of Australia is a federation of six states and two territories each having a considerable degree of independence. Constitutionally, education is the role of the individual State; the Commonwealth Government being limited to co-ordination, leadership and the funding of specific projects. While also considering Australia-wide issues, this paper will concentrate its perspective on the state of Victoria.

In this paper we will provide an overview of the evolution and history of the various streams of educational computing in Australia: University-level Computer Science and Information Systems courses, Primary and Secondary School courses teaching about computing, and the use of computers in other school subjects. Owing to space restrictions, the paper will not address the use of computers in Educational Management at university or school level.

To model the development of the discipline area of Computing we will make use of work by Layton (1972) who wrote on the evolution of subjects within the school curriculum. In Layton's first stage of curriculum development, enthusiastic teachers bring 'missionary enthusiasm' to their task, and justify the new subject on grounds of 'pertinence and utility'. Evolution then occurs into a second stage where a tradition of 'scholarly work' emerges and trained teachers take over its delivery. Greater thought is given to the selection and organisation of subject matter so that this is consistent with the 'internal logic and discipline' of the new subject, rather than just being *useful*. In Layton's third stage complete standardisation, even approaching stagnation, occurs. Subject content is now determined largely by specialist scholars, not on the basis of its utility, and the students have no choice but to accept this (Tatnall, 1993). Although designed to explain evolution of single subjects at the school level we will show how this model can be closely identified in the history of educational computing in Victoria, and applied to the emergence and development of the Computing discipline.

2. UNIVERSITY COMPUTING 1947-1965

In world terms, Australia made its move into computing early. The CSIR Mk1 (CSIRAC), built by Trevor Pearcey and Maston Beard in the late 1940s was Australia's first internally-stored-program computer and is acknowledged to be the world's fourth. Australia had been well placed for an entry into 'the computer age', with a significant manufacturing base for the high technology of the day: the vacuum tube. Combined with expertise in television and radar developed during the 1930s and 1940s this was a critical factor (Pearcey, 1988).

In 1947 the University of Sydney's Department of Mathematics, introduced a course in *The Theory of Computation, Computing Practices, and Theory of Programming* – the first such course in Australia (Pearcey, 1988). At that time, of course, to use a computer at all required knowledge of programming. It was several years before computing was seen anywhere other than statistics and mathematics departments (Pearcey 1988; Tatnall 1992). Programming courses were given regularly in the University of Melbourne from 1956, and in 1959 a subject in *Numerical Methods and Computing* was developed. Undergraduate courses in *Theory of Computation* commenced in 1964 with the establishment of the Department of Information Science (Pearcey, 1988).

In the late 1950s the Commonwealth Government took a decision to computerise the operation of the Department of Defence and the Post Master

General's Department (PMG), creating a massive requirement for trained computing personnel. At this time the universities were only starting to come to grips with the issue of whether computing was a part of mathematics or should be considered as a new discipline. With courses which were quite theoretical in nature, relatively few staff and sparse facilities, the universities were largely unprepared for the demands of the Commonwealth which needed courses with a substantial component that was vocational in nature. The universities had little interest in providing such courses (Tatnall, 1993) so, in 1960 the Australian Government's Commonwealth Public Service Board set up the *Programmers in Training* (PIT) scheme as a temporary measure to alleviate the severe shortage of programmers and other computer professionals in Commonwealth Government departments. The PIT courses were oriented towards training staff for the establishment and running of commercial and administrative computing applications. After several years of operation responsibility for running the PIT courses was transferred completely to the tertiary education sector, and set the style for many of the courses later offered in the Colleges of Advanced Education (CAE)[2].

In the early 1960s, and almost in unison, several key personnel moved from industry to academia to they set up computing courses. Gerry Maynard, coming from the PMG, took up a position at Caulfield Technical College (CTC) and Donald Overheu, from Weapons Research Establishment moved to the University of Queensland. Jack White, Westy Williams and Brian O'Donaghue left the Commonwealth Public Service Board to take positions at CTC, Bendigo Technical College, and RMIT respectively. One of the first educational institutions in Australia to adopt computing as a priority was CTC[3]. As early as 1961 CTC had offered a *Certificate of Accounting (DP)* course and by 1967 the *Diploma of Business Studies (Data Processing)* commenced as what Maynard suggests was the forerunner of many of today's courses in Information Systems. Maynard (1990) claims these courses to be the *first* electronic data processing courses in Australia.

3. COMPUTING BEFORE THE PC: 1965-1977

From 1965 university computing courses became 'respectable' and were soon widely available. In 1969 *Computer Science* was offered in Monash University's science degree. Changes in technology meant that such courses typically moved from delivery on an institution's mainframe to one of its

[2] Australia then had a dual system of tertiary education consisting of Colleges of Advanced Education and a small number of Universities, which later merged to the current Universities.

[3] After a series of amalgamations CTC became a part of Monash University.

new mini-computers producing a fundamental change in the content and availability of computing courses. These courses then proliferated at the Universities and CAEs and by 1975/1977 Monash and Latrobe Universities were offering a Post-Graduate Diploma in *Computer Science*.

It was in the early 1970s that school computing began when a small number of computers started to appear in Australian schools, typically resulting from the exposure of particular teachers to computing during their university studies. In 1972, for example, Burwood High School was loaned a PDP-8 computer by Digital Equipment (Salvas, 1985). In 1973 McKinnon High School received an Innovations Grant to enable the purchase of an 8k Wang computer costing over $10,000 (AUS) and requiring an annual maintenance contract of 15% of the purchase price. Because of this high maintenance cost Box Hill High School agreed to share the use (and costs), each school having access to 4k memory. Box Hill used a Teletype terminal with a paper tape reader and accessed the computer via a dedicated telephone line, but this arrangement was soon seen to be unsatisfactory. These early computers were used by mathematics departments almost exclusively for the teaching of programming (Salvas, 1985).

The biggest impact on schools however, was introduction of the Monash Educational Computer System (MONECS). Before the advent of PC it was impossible for an average school to have hands-on access to a computer. In 1974 a group at Monash University produced a system using mark-sense cards that allowed a class of 30 children to each get two runs in a one-hour period (Monash Computing Museum 2003). The MONECS system was used to teach programming in FORTRAN or BASIC. At this stage schools saw computing as a branch of mathematics concerned with algorithm design.

Another development at this time was experimentation by the Victorian Technical Schools with use of Control Data's 'PLATO System' (PLATO Learning 2004) for computer-assisted instruction for training of apprentices and other possible applications. The system was, however, very expensive and did not proceed. The arrival of the Apple// in 1977 saw the end of this period and the beginning of real advances in the use of computers in schools.

4. IMPACT OF MICROCOMPUTERS: 1977-1990

In this period most of the current computing curriculum in schools and universities was determined. Although some interesting changes occurred in university curriculum at this time, we will concentrate on school computing which the PC made both affordable and useful. We will begin in 1997 when Watsonia High School (where both authors were then teaching) obtained a curriculum innovation grant to purchase an Apple// computer.

4.1 The Advancement of School Computing

In the late 1970s the number of microcomputers in Victorian schools grew rapidly but without any central direction from education authorities. In 1980 Anne McDougall was commissioned to report on how computers were then being used in schools and the possibilities for future use (McDougall 1980). A few years later the Commonwealth Government noted the importance of introducing computers into schools and set up a committee to report on how it might help to provide funding (Commonwealth Schools Commission 1983). One result of the Commonwealth involvement was funds to set up State Computer Education Centres in those states not already having them. These Centres aimed to provide both support and professional development to teachers involved in computer education.

Four streams of computer education soon emerged: Subject use across the curriculum, Computer Science, LOGO, and computer industry/business training in Technical Schools. One of the early curriculum directions was 'computers across the curriculum' and Apple// software like: Lemonade, Hammurabi, and the First Fleet (convict) database showed the possibilities here. Several Subject Associations showed an early interest, particularly the Mathematics, Science and Commercial Teachers' Associations, and a new subject association: the Computer Education Group of Victoria (CEGV) was set up.

4.2 Hardware Brand Wars

There was little software compatibility between the early types of PC used in schools and so it made a big difference to a school's computer education curriculum whether it used Apple//, BBC, Microbee, IBM or Macintosh computers. One of the functions of the State Computer Education Centres was to control the proliferation of these brands by supporting only a limited number on a 'recommended list'. Like several other countries, Australia even commenced a project to design an Australian Educational Computer (Tatnall, 1990), which fortunately (in retrospect) did not proceed past the design stage. Recent developments have seen the rise to dominance in schools of the IBM-compatible PC (Windows) and the Apple Macintosh.

4.3 The Birth and Death of HSC Computer Science

In many school systems the 'worth' of a subject is measured in its interaction with the final year of schooling (Year 12) as many ascribe special importance to those subjects that are seen as valid preparations for tertiary study. In 1981, as a result of many years of effort by a group of academics,

Computer Science was first offered as a Higher School Certificate (HSC) subject in Victoria (Tatnall, 1992). It is interesting to look at reactions to this new subject from tertiary institutions, schools, and the general public. Melbourne and Monash universities, which saw themselves as guardians of academic standards, initially rejected the subject, not allowing its inclusion in admission scores for their courses. Their stated reason for this was that the component of assessment allotted to formal examination was only 35%. When pressed, several academics from these institutions admitted that they considered the subject of little serious academic worth, and 'not an appropriate subject to study at a secondary school level' (Tatnall, 1992). They would often state that they would prefer to have a student with no knowledge of computing whom they could introduce to computing concepts, rather than one 'who had learned bad programming in BASIC'. The fact that the Computer Science subject had been specifically constructed to address this particular concern by the study of top-down design and structured programming missed their notice.

Parallels can be drawn between the introduction of Computer Science and that of Geography in English schools as described by Goodson (1987). An interesting variation is the reaction to the subject by tertiary institutions in Victoria. The 'traditional' universities, which had been offering a highly abstract version of Computer Science for some time opposed introduction of the new subject at secondary school level, claiming that the concepts were above what could be understood by 17-year-old students. The CAEs on the other hand, were generally quite supportive after fighting their own battles with the universities on the place of computing some years earlier.

Parents, students and employers readily accepted HSC Computer Science, and student numbers taking the new subject increased rapidly. Teachers, however, were not universally in favour. Beginning from about the mid-1980s, when Computer Science was still in rapid growth, a number began to question its place. Their arguments had several strands. Firstly, some claimed that Computer Science was an elitist academic subject, too difficult for some students, and so should not be supported (- it is interesting to note that this was exactly opposite to the view earlier held by Melbourne and Monash universities). Others noted that the ratio of girls to boys taking Computer Science was almost as low as that for physics, and expressed concern that it was becoming a *boy's subject*. Perhaps, however, the most damaging criticism came from those teachers who claimed that the presence of a specialist subject detracted from the move to encourage the use of computers *across the curriculum*. Their argument had two parts. Firstly, they argued that the demands made on school computing facilities by Computer Science classes made it difficult for others to obtain adequate access to the machines. While containing some truth, this argument misses the point that in most cases the reason that the school had purchased a number of computers at all was to support the teaching of Computer Science. Secondly, it was argued that the existence of a specialist subject would mean that teachers of other subject areas would not bother to include any mention of computing, considering it covered elsewhere. A number of teachers saw Computer Science and computers *across the curriculum* as adversaries and it took some time before these points of view were reconciled. In 1990, however, changes in the structure of the Year 12 curriculum led to the replacement of *Computer Science* with a much more general subject largely based on PC applications, called *Information Technology*.

5. THE PRESENT: 1990-2004

Changes to the structure of the Year 12 curriculum resulted in the introduction of three new IT subjects: *Information Systems*, *Information Processing and Management* and *Information Technology in Society*. This process also resulted in a decrease in any links between secondary curriculum and the universities. At this time several other subjects were made redundant. A study of particular interest here was *Secretarial Studies* which had been a vocational subject preparing (mostly) girls for entry into office and administrative jobs, but the idea of teaching typing on typewriters was seen as anachronistic. The numerically large and influential number of teachers made redundant in this process produced a pressure group and since these teachers had been moving to electronic typewriters, the best way of occupying them seemed to be to make them IT teachers. This move of Secretarial Studies teachers into Computing can still be seen in the nature and scope of the studies in the final school year.

The 'Computers across the Curriculum' group continued to influence the way computers were used in secondary schools, an interesting example being that of mathematics. In mathematics every year level was required to add computer-based learning of some kind into the curriculum. In 1999 it was found that computing resources in schools were not up to this demand, and a trial at using computers in the examination system failed. Mathematics teachers found the solution to this in relatively inexpensive graphics calculators and use of Excel and Mathematica in schools decreased to zero.

The other phenomenon of the nineties was the Internet and a Government initiative connected all schools to high-speed Internet lines, using a satellite for remote areas. School libraries now boast multiple Internet lines and the Internet intrudes into most social science subjects as a research tool.

6. CONCLUSION

Perhaps because of its early entry, the introduction of computers into all levels of education in Australia occurred very early in a global sense. The story of educational computing has generally followed the path suggested by Layton (1972) and we can see that there have been two important driving forces. The first is the force of the individual: the effect of people like Trevor Pearcey in Universities, and of the MONECS system in high schools can be clearly traced. The second influence is that of government, as initiatives like the funding of teacher training and support units made for rapid progress in computing curriculum. In Victoria, government had an influence through the way it allowed teachers to experiment. Curriculum 'frameworks and guidelines' laid out what students should achieve rather than how to achieve the intended outcomes. This climate of freedom has allowed individuals in schools to develop programs different from many others.

7. REFERENCES

Commonwealth Schools Commission, 1983, Teaching, Learning and Computers. Report of the National Advisory Committee on Computers in Schools. Canberra, Commonwealth Schools Commission

Goodson, I. F., 1987, *School Subjects and Curriculum Change: Studies in Curriculum History - Revised and Extended Edition*. UK, Falmer Press

Layton, D., 1972, "Science as General Education." *Trends in Education, (January)*

Maynard, G., 1990, Personal communication. Melbourne

McDougall, A., 1980, Computers and Post-Primary Education in Victoria: a Study of Needs. Melbourne, Education Department of Victoria

Monash Computing Museum, 2003, Monecs Deamon Educational Computer system. http://www.csse.monash.edu.au/museum/ Feb 2004

Pearcey, T., 1988, *A History of Australian Computing*. Melbourne, Chisholm Institute of Technology

Plato Learning, 2004, History of Plato Learning. Date accessed: Feb 2004, http://www.plato.com/aboutus/company_history.asp

Salvas, A. D., 1985, Personal communication. Melbourne

Tatnall, A., 1990, "Designing the Australian Educational Computer." *Education* **110**(4): 453-456

Tatnall, A., 1992, The Growth of Educational Computing in Australia. *History, Context, and Qualitative Methods in the Study of Education*. Goodson, I., F. and Mangan M. J. London, Ontario, University of Western Ontario, Canada. **Vol 3: 207-248**

Tatnall, A., 1993, A Curriculum History of Business Computing in Victorian Tertiary Institutions from 1960 - 1985. *MA thesis*. Deakin University.

GROWTH OF COMPUTING TECHNOLOGY FOR EDUCATION IN INDIA

Rakesh Mohan Bhatt
HNB Garhwal University, India
Email: rmbhatt@edumail.nic.in

Abstract: Education and expansion of education have been the main task of any society. Owing to its heterogeneity and pressure from a population of over one billion, India needs more rigorous attempts to elevate its education status; though some of its parts are well socially developed. Further, with the deployments of computers in the educational institutions and infrastructural developments to meet the computer enabled services, remarkable growth has been observed. While discussing the status of the growth of computing technology for education, emerging computing and infrastructural environments and other related developments have also been discussed in this paper.

Key words: Computing technology; India; Education

1. INTRODUCTION

History of Indian education has witnessed several endeavors and many changes in the educational system. The ancient Indian educational system was based on the Gurukul concept where the mode and contents of learning were decided by the teacher, the Guru himself. At that time we did not have any kind of professional or job centric education. During India's pre-independence period, a separate Department of Education was established in 1910. At the time of independence on 15th August 1947, India had a population of 350 million. A Ministry of Education was established on 29th August 1947. Between the years1950-1951 to 2001-2002, the growth of enrollment in primary, upper primary, secondary and senior secondary has increased by 6, 14 and 20 times. Similarly, the number of colleges for general education and professional education has also increased by about 24 and 12 times respectively; while the number of universities has increased by 10 times during the period 1950-1951 to 2001-2002 [1]. The percent of education expenditure to GDP in 1991-1992 was 0.64 only which is now 4.04 in 2001-2002.

Influenced by the advancement in science and technology, educational institutions encourage the use of new learning modes to achieve their goals. Computing in education is increasingly becoming a vital tool and computers have dominated its role. This is the main focus of this paper besides discussing the phenomenal growth of other media/technology, viz. radio, television, video, teleconferencing, Internet, and communication infrastructure.

2. THE PHENOMENAL GROWTH IN COMPUTING TECHNOLOGY

Computing technology in education can be understood as comprised of different media and technology to interact with society for educational purposes. It may cover one or more of: a) Media and AV communication, e.g., alternative instructional delivery systems such as Radio, ETV, etc.; b) Training tools like CBT (Computer Based Training) and CAD (computer-aided design), etc.; c) Instructional delivery and management via computers and computer-based systems, e.g. CAI (Computer Assisted Instruction) etc.; and d) Internet/web based education.

The following sections discuss the beginning of the computing era in India, its entry in the education systems and other developments.

2.1 The Foundation Era

The first computer came to India in 1965 and was used in the Indian industry. This entry was observed as a replacement of the mechanical tabulators [2]. Education in computer science began at Indian Institute of Technology, Kanpur, and the first Ph.D. graduated in 1969. About 2000 working professionals were also produced by this institute during 1970s. Further, during this period, for the first time in India, Electronics Corporation of India Ltd. (ECIL) designed a machine TDC-12 (Trombay Digital Computer-12), but could not provide its viable stay in the market [3]. For promoting education in information technology (IT), post B.Sc. and Master of Computer Applications (MCA) were recommended by the man power committee which became functional around 1980s. The design of mini-computers by Indian companies also accrued during this period [4]. During 1980s, the demand for IT education and growth in software industry were observed. Around 1990s, the general public saw the application of computers in a broader way when Computer Maintenance Corporation Ltd. (CMC) computerized the reservation system of the Indian railways; the happening allayed the fear of unemployment as conceived earlier [3]. During this period, Indian software professionals got world-wide recognition. In 1995, internet was available access for the Indian public. After 1996, each year, about 45% annual growth of computer PCs was observed. In August 1997, Indian economists observed (Computer@home, Feb. 2001, Cyber Media (India) Ltd., www.dqindia.com) the knowledge-based industries at a new threshold in India that grew faster than any other infotech industry in the world. Since then many milestones have been crossed.

2.2 Primary and Secondary Education

Presently, the formal education system covers over 106 million children at primary stage, 39 million at middle stage and 23 million at secondary stage [5]. For diffusion of information for education, on 28th October 1961, televisions were provided in the schools, for the first time in India. The satellite instructional television experiment (SITE) was conducted [6] from August 1975 to July 1976. After its success, many satellites were launched and direct broadcast proved [7] cheaper than the conventional system. Further, countrywide classroom programs were started [8] on 15th August 1984. CLASS (Computer Literacy and Studies in Schools) and CLAP (Computer Literacy and Awareness Programme) were also launched during 1984. A total of 12,000 such Computers were received and distributed to Secondary and Senior Secondary Schools through State Governments. "Operation blackboard" was also launched in 1987 and 23000 schools were covered. For the development of education in its entirety, the updated Programme of Action (POA) in 1992 under the National Policy on Education (NPE), 1986, enunciated a comprehensive framework. Following this, decentralization in education was done through the local bodies – the Panchayat Raj institutions. To promote quality and modern education, 503 Jawahar Navodaya Vidyalayas (a kind of special schools from VI to XII level) for the rural children, were opened in almost every district of the country. NPE also emphasizes the use of multimedia packages and related technologies. During 1995-1996, National Council of Educational Research and Training (NCERT) also conducted an experiment on audio and video conferencing. Other experiments using the computing technologies have recorded positive effects on motivation among the variety of target groups of the learners.

The Project CLASS was further continued under governmental five year plans, under which, 2598 schools having BBC Micros were equipped under this project. In addition, 2371 schools were also covered with new hardware and services. Further, to address the new vision and long-term objectives, the scheme was stopped in 1996-1997 and renamed as CLASS 2000. The revised scheme started in 2001-2002 and proposed to choose 10,000 schools to provide computer literacy and another 1000 schools to provide computer-based learning. Under the concept of Smart Schools, choosing 100 schools as a pace setters, was envisaged. Therefore, under this total literacy campaign (TLC) during last year in 2003, out of total 588 districts in the country, more than 550 districts have been covered and the rest are in the ongoing phase [9].

2.3 Higher Education

For the higher-level education, University Grants Commission (UGC) is the apex body vested with the responsibility of development of higher education in the country. It has been providing financial assistance to all Central, State and Deemed Universities, both under Plan and Non-Plan schemes, for improving infrastructure and basic facilities. Presently, 294 universities/ institutions in India have 13150 affiliated colleges, about 8.8 million students, and 430000 teachers [1]. About 142 university libraries are on the way to computerization [10]. In the late 1970s, RECs (regional engineering colleges) and private colleges were opened [11]. To further boost the growth of technical higher education, in 1992, AICTE (All India Council for Technical Education) and some other institutions were established. It was decided on 1 November 2001, to establish "A UGC Network" for providing information connectivity to each university, UGC has now started the UGC INFONET for the virtual enhancement of the academic structure. By the beginning of 2004, about 183 universities are being covered under this network.

Need of continuing education and for equal opportunity for higher education, of the developments in the field of information communication technology and of enhancement of infrastructure for communication, have generated excellent opportunity. In view of this, Indira Gandhi National Open University (IGNOU) established during late eighties, offers 72 programmes and its cumulative enrolment in 2001 stood at over 1.2 million. The University has created a network of student support-structure, with 46 regional centers and 765 study centers all over the country. The University has also created a media network and teleconferencing system to electronically link all distance-teaching institutions in the country. Many earlier departments of correspondence courses in various universities have been converted into independent open universities during the ninth plan period. There are, at present, nine open universities in the country, all founded by different states during the nineties.

To measure the role and impact of computing technologies, some significant experiments were conducted. Some of them are discussed here. IGNOU conducted a Cable TV network programme in April 1993 through interactive mode [12], another in October 1993 covering its 10 regional canters through teleconferencing mode [13]. The programme recorded a positive response from the participants. Another telecourse was conducted [14] over television by Consortium for Educational Communication (CEC) between 15-24 December ember 1994 The revised educational technology scheme in 1987 gave emphasis over TV and audio program production-capabilities and its wider access on TV and radio-come-cassette players (RCCP).The Central Institute of Educational Technology (CIET) started Class-2000 on Door-Darshan channel on 50:50 basis [15].

To supplement the face-to-face academic counseling through All India Radio (AIR) and over 1620 radio lessons were broadcasted until 2000. Interactive radio-phone started on 23rd April 2000. Telecast of the Video lesson took place from 1st November 1999. Interactive teleconferencing, a part of education technology conducted on 14 and 15 March 1999 and in the year 2000 over 20 such conferences took place [16].

2.4 Infrastructural Developments

Telecommunications is one of the prime support services needed for rapid growth and modernization of various sectors of the economy. It has become especially important in recent years because of enormous growth of Information Technology (IT) and a significant impact on the rest of the economy. India is perceived to have a special comparative advantage in IT and in IT-enabled services. During the Ninth Plan period, a record growth rate of telecom services was achieved in the country. The network (equipped capacity) grew at an average rate of about 22%. Current efforts involve approval of the Convergence Bill 2000; Internet Telephony has also been opened from 1st April 2002. In 1995, India started its cellular phone service and now the base of the cellular network has grown only 0.34 million connections to 6.43 million connections by the year 2002. As per the Telecom Regulatory Authority of India (TRAI), the mobile subscriber base is expected (www.trai.gov.in) to grow from 30 million of the year 2003 to 55 million mark in 2004. Growth of the tele-density has become 4.4 as of 31 March 2002 (tripled as on 1997). It is envisaged that the country need to achieve an overall tele-density of 9.91 by the end of the Tenth Plan i.e. March 2007 [17].

In the present status of Telecom services Network, the total of fixed telephone connections is 38.60 million. Internet Connections are 4 million now [18]. Presently, 17 million people are using the Internet [19]. 70 million households have TV and 35 million have the cable connection.

2.5 Initiatives in IT sector

Government notification on 25th July 1998 recommended 108 points of improvement [20] by the national task force on IT and software development which was set up on 22nd May 1998 to formulate the draft of a national informatics policy. The WG on IT for masses [21] was constituted by government on 10th May 2000. The group deliberated on issues like infrastructure and service, èlectronic governance, education, and mass campaign for IT awareness. Among the 16 points, the education related issues are: IT in government, Citizen IT interface, IT spread and IT awareness. The Media Lab Asia project has also been initiated in 2001 to make IT popular for the masses. Upgradation of the Education and Research Network (ERNET) connecting various universities and regional engineering colleges (RECs) through a high speed network is on the way. Further, for bridging the digital divide, 487 Community Information Centers at the block headquarters in the northeastern states and Sikkim is being set-up. The Ministry of IT has envisaged in its IT Action plan increase 100 million internet connections by 2008 with a ratio of one PC per 50 people. To provide legal recognition for transactions through electronic data interchange, the Information Technology (IT) Act, 2000, has already been enacted. Spending for IT is about 0.7% of GDP. As per NASSCOM [22], spending for IT was increased by 24% during 2003. With the growth of over 60% in the ITES sector during the year 2002-2003, NASSCOM [23] estimated its growth of US $21-24 billion by 2008.

In view of the on-going development, it is noteworthy that there has been significant increase in the government plan outlays for computer/internet connections and its training in education; telecommunication, information and broadcasting sectors, so these efforts will certainly enhance the computing technology for education in India. In the following section, the efforts which accelerate the growth are discussed.

3. ACCELERATIVE EFFORTS

Interestingly, computers have been in use for about 25 to 30 years in India but only by English educated citizens. In India, 18 languages and 10 different scripts are recognized and about 1650 dialects used in the various states. This may be one of the reasons for the low penetration rate of PCs which is only 6 per 100. To improve this situation to date, ISCII (Indian Script Code for Information Interchange) and Unicode standards have been evolved [24] to allow the simultaneous use of English and script alphabets, and to encode the multilingual text respectively. During the tenth five year plan (2002-2007), Vidyavahani and Gyan Vahini projects were started [25] on a pilot basis for providing connectivity to government senior secondary schools and higher learning institutions, respectively. A portal developed under the Vidhyanidhi project [26] helps doctoral research through a pedagogic journey, very exiting and rich with its facilities, resources and tools. 25-30% of the doctoral theses in India are in local languages, Vidyavahini uses Unicode for its digital library of local language e-theses. Another project, Gyan Nidhi [25] aims to develop a 1 million page multilingual parallel corpus in English and 12 Indian languages.

Keeping in view the current demand for IT and computerization, a major thrust has been noticed to familiarize students with information technology. The State Governments are preparing Computer Education Plans (CEP). The scheme "ICT in Schools" include - i) strengthening and reorientation of staff, ii) digitization of SIETs' video and audio cassettes on the basis of need assessment and in partnership with NGOs, iii) web/internet based education to be managed by the SIETs, and iv) production of video and audio cassettes after assessing the demand.

Many web-sites offer open on-line debates on how to popularize the education among children. For example, Vidya On-line [27] invites teachers, researchers, academics and concerned individuals to participate in the on-line forum, particularly on issues related with the ICT for education in primary education.

The Act 2002 was enacted for free and compulsory education as a fundamental right for all children between 6-14 in December 2002. To promote computer literacy, the department of IT has also constituted computer literacy excellence award for schools. More than 1000 pilot projects are running by GOI for spreading IT among the masses. About Rs. 14550 million have been spent in these projects [28]. The success rate is estimated at 40%.

To further remove the drawback present in the education system and to elevate its status, national education policy was updated in 1992, decentralized education, emphasized micro-planning, and Village Education

Committees. Afterwards, many innovative programmes are implemented like the Special Orientation Programme (SOP) which was the first experiment using interactive TV conducted from 7-13 January 1986 and was found [29] in favor of the learner. Further initiatives are Sarva Shiksha Abhiyan at the national level and at state level are Lok Jumbish, Bihar Educational Project, and Andra Pradesh Educational Programme etc. In these programmes, during 1992-1993 to 1995-1996, Rs. 8163 million and during 1996-1997, Rs. 2910 million were spent. The aim, to maintain the presence of about 200 million children throughout their courses and to sustain their integration in further classes, is yet to be achieved. To send every child to school during the year 2003 Rs. 54500 million were sanctioned and in the current year Rs. 30000 million has been allocated [30].

IGNOU has established the Distance Education Council (DEC) to act as the nodal agency for the distance education system at the tertiary level. The university has adopted an integrated multimedia instructions strategy consisting of print material and audio-video programmes, supported by counseling sessions at study centers throughout the country. A dedicated Satellite TV Channel, Gyan Darshan, managed by IGNOU, is beaming educational programmes from school to tertiary level 24 hours a day. Preparations are on to launch 40 FM educational radio channels (Gyan Vani) in the country under a Memorandum of Understanding with Prasar Bharati. During the Tenth Plan, IGNOU would set up open universities in States, which presently do not have them, and to expand the activities of Gyan Darshan and Gyan Vani in different parts of the country. The target is to extend the coverage of open learning systems to backward regions, remote inaccessible areas of the northeast, and low female literacy blocks in some of the eastern states. Courses have also been offered through the virtual campus of IGNOU [31] and Tamil Virtual University. Some recent experiments are being conducted to measure its role and dimensions. Some of them are discussed in the following section.

4. OTHER EXPERIMENTS

In an attempt at IIT Kanpur, a teleconferencing tool [32], consisting of three components, the teacher, the students' console and the lecture manager, is designed to allow the teacher to present lectures using text, viewgraphs, graphics, audio and video files. Interaction can take place via a whiteboard or by speaking up. In the learning environment, method of transmission of information is the most important element as a content-carrier between teacher and student. To enable the virtual environment, where the teacher/student is projected distantly, a software prototype design - Virtual

Lecture Hall, have been developed. This is a part of the project Virtual Classroom at IIT Kanpur that aims to provide virtual education and training, preserving simultaneously the norms of the lecture hall. Designing a virtual learning environment for situated learning, IIT Kharagpur, has evolved a system [33] in the form of the ElNet-3L (Electronically Networked Life-Long-Learning) project which disseminate the course in the Tutored Video Instruction (TVI) mode through the 'Collaborative Group Learning' format. It is also reported [34] to use the upgraded communication switches and facilities to enhance the course effectiveness. Computer-based and computer mediated collaborative learning model are also being developed at the ER and DCI, Calcutta [35], to provide computer assistance for remote learning based on the principles of Instruction Design propagated by Robert Gagne. Very recently, a satellite, EduSet, has been set [36] to launch in 2004 with aims to educate the Indian masses from all streams of life.

5. IMPLICATIONS

Several of the above mentioned experiments have been observed. Their implications will be discussed here. One of the success stories is from Gyandood project [37]. It was implemented in the Dhar district of MP state, where cyber café-come-cyber offices for masses as well as social engineering through IT were introduced. Its success was adjudged on many dimensions and the project received the prestigious award- Stockholm challenge - IT Award-2000 on 6th June 2000. In another project, the Simputer Trust [38] a non-profit trust created basically to develop technology that will help take information technology to rural areas has been started. It has developed "Simputer", a new cheap computer for the poor. Its initial target is India. The visually impaired can use the video camera to scan text. The optical character recognition software converts it into text that a computer can understand, and then text software converts that text into audible speech. Thus a blind person could now read.

Indian industries felt that bridging up the existing digital divide exists in the community will in turn give success to their business. Past years have seen many fruitful initiatives in IT literacy campaigns. The detail stories of the companies like IBM, NIIT, Aptech, Infosys, Xansa, Intel, Cisco and Texas Instruments can be found on-line [39], where IT literacy has been discussed as the new social cause.

Set-up in 2003, the INDEST Consortium (Indian National Digital Library in Engineering Sciences and Technology), has subscribed to over 5000 electronic journals [40] and any institute can become informational rich in promoting advances in teaching and learning process.

6. DISCUSSION

As a result of the ongoing effort, significant results can be noticed e.g. during 1961 to 1996, fall in drop-out rates from 70% to 40% have been found in the primary schools children. In 1991, the literacy rate was 52.21% and made up to 65.37% in 2001. UNESCO reports also shows 30% increase to access the basic education, which might show the impact of the input of computing technology in education.

Measures to increase enrolment, including that of the disadvantaged sections, in the higher education system would be given utmost attention. It is hoped that role of computing technology can give a raise of 4% in the enrolment of the age group 18-23 as envisaged [41] during the years 2002-2007. A major catalyzing factor has been the dynamism and enthusiasm of the Government in the planning and deployment of Information Technology (IT) in schools. Institutions such as UGC, IGNOU, and CIET have started to transmit the curriculum on Doordarshan channel, but the ETV's education specific programmes do not meet the demand of the students [42]. In changing the instruction design in the current paradigm, IT means can have a major impact on teaching and learning processes.

7. CONCLUSION

The on-going implementation of the computing technologies for education could create a suitable learning environment, required for the group as well as student-centric learning environment. One of the main advantages of such an environment is the flexibility that leads to make the size to fit into one's learning needs or acquisition of knowledge. Therefore, educational institutes should meet the required changes/ upgrading to provide the need based computing technologies. Many efforts have established this technology as a self-support system to meet the varied requirements and to enhance the quality of educational practices by increasing self-initiation, self-motivation, self-reliance etc. Thus, we hope, in the bright sunny years to come, this silver lining of the computing technologies will grow in many folds in length and width in finding new education possibilities by providing new openings and opportunities to learn.

ACKNOWLEDGEMENTS

I sincerely acknowledge the valuable suggestions from the HCE Program Committee and others to reconstructing the paper in the present shape. I also sincerely acknowledge the encouragement received from N. Natarajan, Vice-Chancellor, HNB Garhwal University, and Srinagar. I am also grateful to D. R. Purohit for his careful proof-reading. I am also grateful to the Computer Society of India for their support.

REFERENCES

1. http://www.education.nic.in/htmlweb/higedu.htm.01-10-2001. National Infomatics Centre.
2. Prasad, Kamta and Verma, Pramod. Impact of Computer on Employment, New Delhi: McMillan Co., 1976.
3. Rajaraman,V. "IT in India-A Retrospective (1965-99)".CSI Communication,Jan.2000:.9-14.
4. "Report of the panel on computer man power development (Chairman Prof. V. Rajaraman) Electronics information and planning". Information and planning group, Government of India. 8. November1980:.55-70.
5. Elementary Education.01-10-2001. National Informatics Centre. 23-3-2004. http://www.education.nic.in/htmlweb/main.htm/eleedu1.htm.
6. Sharma ,D. K.." Distance education systems of the future". University News .24(42).(1986): 55-57.
7. Nath, Ram." Space technology in the third world and towards strategy of self reliance". University. News. 21(1).(1983):.2-5.
8. Booklet on UGC countrywide classroom,.
9. Literacy in India.23-07-2003.Commonwealth of Learning. 30-12-2003. http://www.col.org /literacy/india/htm.
10. http://web.inflibnet.ac.in.25-02-2004.Informational Library Network, An Autonomous Institute of UGC
11. Dutta, Rattan K ."Bridging order in chaotic IT education" .CSI Communication, January 2004 :5-9.
12. Chaudhari,Sohanvir S.,and ihari, Sham. "Modasa experiment: distance teaching through cable TV". IJOL 3(1)1994:24-28.
13. Sahoo, P. K., 1994. "Teleconferencing in distance education : IGNOU experiment". IJOL 3(1)(1994):31.
14. New communication and information technologies (a tele-conference course package) CEC, New Delhi. 1994.
15. Khullar, K. K. "Electronic programme - missing target groups". ***The hindustan times, news paper.*** 8 August 1995.
16. Khanam, Shakeela. "Learning in future", University News, 8(47), 2000.
17. Planning Commission. 10-05-2003. National Informatics Centre. 23-3-2004. http://planningcommission.nic.in/plans/planrel/fiveyr/welcome.html.
18. Amar Ujjala News paper. 04 Feb. 2004.
19. Zee News Channel. 25-09-03. 8.30pm.
20. Information Technology.03-07-2001.Ministryof IT, Government of India. 23-2-2004. http://it-taskforce.nic.in.
21. IT for Masses. 24-6-2000. National Infomatics Centre.23.2.2004. www.itformasses.nic.in.
22. Express Computer,.13(44). 2003.
23. Singh , Nikita, "IT careers for you". CSI Communication, January, 2004:13-16.

24. Fichardo, Chris Ann. "The A AA E of Indic computing", *Express Computer*, 15 Sept. 2003:14-16.
25. http://www.cdacindia.com. 12-9-2003. Ministry of IT, Government of India.
26.Urs, Shalini R.Vidyanidhi, "Digital Library and E-Scholarship", Portal.25-09-2003. http://www.vidyanidhi.org.in
27. Discussion Forum. 27-12-2003. Dept. of Education, Ministry of Human Resource & Development. http://www.vidyaonline.net/
28. Latest Trivia.07-11-2003. www.bhashaindia.com/trivia/trivia.aspx
29. Das,NK."Reaction of primary school teachers towards training through interactive TV". *IJOL*, 6(2) (1997):.77-90.
30. Bamjai, Kavery. India Today. Feb.17-23, 2004:44.
31. Indira Gandhi National Open University. 24-07-2003. http://www.ignou.edu
32. Manjunath, D, Sale, Sandhya V. and Tripathi, Madhu."Remote Tutor - A multimedia Teleseminaring Tool for an Internet"., Int'l conf. on Collaborative and Networked Learning, 16-18 Feb. 1998:58-62.
33. Komaragiri,Vihari V. and Sanghi Dheeraj, "Designing a virtual learning environment for situated learning", Int'l conf. on Collaborative and Networked Learning.16-18 Feb.1998:.71-75.
34. Bhattacharya, B and Roy ,A. K. "Off-Campus Distance Education through Electronically Networked Study Centre". Int'l conf. on Collaborative and Networked Learning.16-18 Feb.1998: 45-49.
35. Saha, Amiya Baran, SenGupta ,Suparna, and Jain,Deepak."Computer Assisted Learning: A New Approach by ERandDCI Calcutta" National Centre for Software Technology. http://www.ncst.ernet.in/vidyakash2002/extra-papers/Computer_Assisted_Learning-A_New_Approach.doc
36. National Institute of Eduaction & Planning. 22-05-2003. http://www.niepaonline.org /whatsnew.htm
37. Rajora , Rajesh and Vyas, Nitesh. "Gyandoot".CSI communication.Feb. 2001:13-14.
38. India's simple computer for poor.24-09-2001.British Broadcasting Company.26-11-2004. http://news.bbc.co.uk/1/hi/sci/tech/1560771.stm.
39.Jasrotia, Punita.IT literacy – the newsocial cause. http://www.expressitpeople.com /20020318/cover.html. 18March.2002.
40. http://paniit.iitd.ac.in/indest. 25-9-2003. Indian Institute of Technology.
41. http://www.ciet.nic.in/etissues.html. 23-05-2002. Central Institute of Eduactional Technology.
42. Rai, K and Bhattacharya, P.K. "Implications of IT for teacher education and research". http://www.ciet.nic.in/etissues.html. 03-08-2002.Central Institute of Educational Technology.

COMPUTING AND EDUCATION IN THE UK

The First Twenty Years

Jennifer Davies
University of Wolverhampton, UK
E-mail: J.Davies2@wlv.ac.uk

Abstract: Computing arose as a numerically significant occupational area in industrialised nations after the Second World War. The right economic conditions for it to become established were met first in the US; the economies of Western Europe and Japan being about ten years behind. By the 1950s jobs in computing were perceived as occupations with some status but, by the Millennium, commentators had realised that computing had failed to professionalise.

Set against this background, this paper describes developments in computing education in the UK at further and higher education level from 1960 until the 1980s. It is from the perspective of the professional body for computing in the UK as recorded in the British Computer Society (BCS) publication, *Computer Bulletin*. This paper argues that three drivers impacted on the computing curriculum in the UK. First, the British Government was concerned about the health of the British computer industry and future skills shortages. Second, the educational establishments were responding to immediate demand, driven by the employers and potential students. Third, the BCS was seeking to establish itself as the professional body for computing in the UK.

In conclusion, this paper demonstrates that the evolution and growth of the system of computing education in the UK at further and higher education level, from the early 1960s to the late 1980s, was a synergistic response on the part of the educational institutions to the requirements of the British Government, industry and commerce and the professional body, the BCS.

Key words: Computing education; Further education; Higher education; Professional body; Government support; Industry; UK.

1. INTRODUCTION

Government support for industry may take several forms and those that meet favour vary with time and between nations depending, for instance, upon the political persuasion of the government in power and national culture. Educational programs may form one facet of industrial policy. (Brandin and Harrison, 1987) Most of the expenditure on computing technology in the US in the 1950s was for military objectives; the commercial computing sector in the US was sustained financially during this period by the US armed forces and defence industry, bolstered by the strength of the US economy (Cordata, 1997). During the 1950s Britain invested a fraction of the amount the US did in military contracts for computing technology, £12m as against £350m (Owen, 1999). In Britain, by the late 1950s, the developing computing industry was losing to US competition from IBM. The increasing dominance of the high technology sector by US multinational corporations prompted concern, so that when Harold Wilson won the British general election in 1964 he established a Ministry of Technology, Mintech, a key feature of the remit of which was to save the British computer industry (Campbell-Kelly, 1995). This was to be through British government support of a national champion, ICL. Throughout the 1970s and 1980s ICL was fighting for its survival against IBM, bailed out by a succession of governments, because of the perceived acute strategic significance of computing to the future of the British economy. Another facet of the British government's considerable support for its computing industry was its involvement in the education of computer personnel, the need for which became apparent in the early 1960s. For instance, the Robbins Committee on Higher Education reported to the British Computer Society (BCS) in 1962 that there was a serious shortage of qualified, advanced technicians able to maintain computer equipment (The Editor, 1962).

2. DEVELOPMENTS

In 1967 Buckingham (1967) reviewed the progress that had been made in computing education over the previous five years. He observed that, in that period, it had evolved rapidly from a position of no discernible widespread system to a nascent organisation based on numbers and types of personnel required and appropriate curricula. Earlier, in 1960, the remit of a two-day conference held at Hatfield Technical College, on the Computing Laboratory in the Technical College, was the effect of computing machines on the discipline of mathematics. Barritt (1960) defined categories of technical college students then as commercial background, scientists, electronic engineers, programmers, operators and various types of mathematicians.

- Students from commerce benefit from the lavish use of flow-charts;
- Scientists – immediate application to formulae drawn from their own work is helpful;
- Programmers – can safely work through the manufacturer's manual.

Wegner (1963), in reporting three years later, on another two-day conference on computer education held at Hatfield Technical College described the efforts at that time as *ad hoc.* He lamented that the most common attitude to computer education was that computers were a tool whose use should be learnt through vocational training at technical colleges, rather than their study in itself providing an intellectual challenge. Nonetheless, in the critical recognition of an industrial/commercial perspective, the situation had progressed from that of 1960. In the following year, a representative of the Royal Insurance Group, Hughson (1964) reported the difficulty he had experienced in finding suitable day release courses for computer staff employed in commercial data processing centres. He deplored the lack of courses provided by higher education (HE) that would provide "a good commercial/technical education with special attention to computers and associated business techniques".

In his review, Buckingham (1967) summarised a government report estimating the number of computer staff required by 1970. These figures refer to the needs of industry and commerce and ignore those of educational institutions.

Table 1. Projected increase in number of computer staff required by 1970 (From Buckingham, 1967, p. 6)

Type	Numbers in 1964	Additions needed by 1970
Advanced programmers	Not specified	200
Systems designers	3,600	500
Systems analysts	3,600	11,000
Programmers	4,800	19,200
Operators	3,000	16,000
Maintenance staff	2,500 – 3,000 (in 1965)	Not specified

It was assumed that advanced programmers and systems designers were of honours degree standard, systems analysts were of "graduate quality" and that the other types of staff were technical grades. Furthermore, despite the large increase required in the numbers of technical grade staff, it was felt that their training did not pose a problem as it could probably be dealt with by the computer manufacturers, such as English Electric-Leo. This company provided specialist training for their customers' staff as well as for their own needs, their major effort being in the training of programmers, operators and maintenance engineers (Gibson, 1964). The significant issue was seen by the government to be the education of systems analysts and designers. The government report produced a number of recommendations, emphasising that a high priority should be given to training systems analysts and the implications for universities, further education (FE) colleges and the National Computing Centre (NCC). For the universities, they recommended the involvement of the computer manufacturers in curriculum development, more computer facilities allocated for teaching purposes, rejigging some courses towards system design, and increased grant provision. For further education colleges the recommendations focussed on reviewing and augmenting existing provisions.

Buckingham (1967) reviewed the existing and estimated higher education and further education provision to meet this projected demand. At that time the development of post-graduate courses in computing was ahead of that of undergraduate. This was because it had until then been uncertain whether computer science represented an acceptable academic discipline. More exactly, computing related topics were perceived as evolving, experimental new fields of study, with indistinct boundaries and, as such, more suitably placed within postgraduate diploma or masters level courses. The majority of post-graduate courses had developed from the study of numerical analysis at older universities and by 1967 included such topics as theory of computation, symbol manipulation, compilers and data structures. Buckingham hoped that more than 500 students would have received such an award by 1970. He also estimated that there was an additional but significantly lower number of students who were undertaking post-graduate research in computer science or registering for new diploma and MSc courses in data processing and systems analysis.

By 1967, computer science was becoming established as an academic subject at undergraduate level. Six colleges of technology formed the majority of the vanguard in offering courses predominantly concerned with the theory and use of computers, in their case validated by the Council for National Academic Awards (CNAA) and incorporating an industrial year. This trend mirrored the establishment of engineering as an academic subject in Britain in the nineteenth century. Cambridge did not establish a chair in engineering until 1875 and Oxford not until 1907, despite fears of Continental superiority (Sviedrys, 1970), although the civic universities gained chairs earlier, endowed by industrialists, for example Manchester in 1867. Additionally, by 1967 eight universities were offering joint degree courses where computer science was the most significant component. Buckingham estimated that by 1970 undergraduate courses would be supplying more than 350 graduates per year, who had studied a course with a substantial computer science component, and that figure was increasing.

Table 2. Estimated supply of computer science graduates by 1970 (From Buckingham, 1967, p. 8)

Institution	First year 1965/66	First year 1967/68	Graduates by 1970
Colleges of Technology	104	213	250 – 300
Universities			100+
Total			350+

Samet (1968) contrasted the attitude of the universities with that of the technical colleges in meeting the educational requirements of personnel aspiring to become data processing managers. He believed that the universities were doing far too little, being concerned with teaching mathematically based topics. "Commerce and industry are not really respectable." He felt that the technical colleges were ahead of the universities as their courses possessed "a practical outlook" and "wide background".

Buckingham thought that the further education colleges should be meeting the need for technical grade personnel. The City and Guilds of London Institute (C&G) had been engaged in technical education since 1878. In 1962, the BCS requested its involvement in computer education for junior personnel within the existing further education structure. C&G's *Certificate for Computer Personnel,* a two-year part-time course, launched in 1964, was first examined in 1966, and is believed to be the first formal examination in computer studies held by a recognised body. The objective of the two-stage course, of which the Certificate formed the first stage, was to enrich the in-service training and experience of junior programmers, so that the knowledge they gained enabled them to program a computer more effectually. The second stage developed them to be fully competent programmers, ready to assume positions of responsibility. Colleges offering the course had to be approved by C&G; nine colleges gaining approval in 1964. By 1968 the number had risen to 60. (Stevens, 1969) In 1966, 62 candidates passed the Certificate, that number had risen to 368 in 1968 with 480 projected for 1969.

In 1967 part-time Higher National Certificate (HNC) and full-time Higher National Diploma (HND) courses were becoming established (Buckingham, 1967) so that by 1970 27 institutions were offering Higher National Certificate or Higher National Diploma courses in Computer

Studies at sub-degree level (BCS, 1970). Furthermore, encouraging noises had been made about an Ordinary National Certificate which would allow students to progress to a Higher National Certificate, as early as 1962 (Barritt, 1962) although these proposals were deferred until the 1970s. The establishment of the Technician Education Council (TEC) in 1973 and the Business Education Council (BEC) in 1974, under the auspices of the Secretary of State for Education and Science, led to the creation of the BEC/TEC Computer Studies Committee in 1977 with responsibility for "the development of a nationally recognised integrated framework of courses in non-degree further education and higher education leading to awards in Computer Studies". (Staple and Shaw, 1981) By September 1980, about 80 colleges were providing BEC/TEC National Certificate or Diploma courses in Computer Studies. When, in 1986, the course underwent a revision to take account of technological developments, there were more than 250 centres with an annual intake in excess of 4500. (Buckingham, 1986)

In 1975 Simpson and Kerridge (1975) reviewed part-time education in computing, which they classified as day release, evening courses for professional body qualifications, or at the level of computer appreciation, and specialist one week blocks requested by industry. Day release, for example for Higher National Certificate, was the least popular option. They concluded, based on their own experience, that producing a coherent system of part-time provision would be very difficult as such a system would have to cater for differences in technical level of the students, differences in their ability to attend college, as well as differences in their objectives in attending the course. It would also have to be able to incorporate intermittent requests from industry for special courses. This was despite a high national requirement for trained first entry computer personnel, a need to up-skill existing staff, and the desire by non-computer specialists for a computer qualification.

During the 1970s a process of consolidation took place at higher education level with some debate over the structuring of degree courses (Joubert and Stander, 1970) and the mathematical bias of university courses in computer science (Colin, 1971). Moreton (1977), in his review, noted that computer science had become recognised as an academic discipline with over 40 first degree courses. However, he drew attention to an issue that was then causing concern, lack of compatibility of many university courses of study with what employers expected graduates to know, but he argued that computer science courses were evolving to meet the needs of industry for skilled personnel. Day (1974) earlier described the "unsolved problem of computer science ... how are those who want practical training going to get it?" He was referring to university courses that, in aiming for academic respectability, were failing to teach programming techniques soundly, as programming was viewed as containing little intellectual content. Further he stated that undergraduates had no practice in applying their knowledge to large, real world problems.

Addressing this issue, Penney (1975) reported on the progress made by a BCS working party set up in 1972 to consider the curriculum of a degree in data processing, which prepared the graduate "to make an immediate contribution to the everyday work of a data processing department", to provide management in business, commerce and administrative departments with reliable, timely and relevant information. The proposed curriculum contained technical topics such as computer systems and programming systems as well as areas like social and organisational studies. The proposals were criticised by King (1976) as representing a joint degree in the subjects of computer science and business administration. King suggested that students should study for a degree in computer science and take specialist routes later in their curriculum. Notwithstanding such criticisms, following the publication of the BCS report (Land, 1975) and as a result of it, a number of degree courses in data processing were established.

Bell and Robson (1985) reviewed a course in data processing which had been established at Sunderland Polytechnic in 1979 as a consequence of the BCS report, and concluded that the curriculum the report contained had been proved to be "both appropriate and robust", merely requiring fine tuning. This was despite developments in microprocessor technology in the US in the early 1970s having provided the basis for the production of the microcomputer, and having initiated massive computer-based changes in business and society in the intervening years.

Another change, brought about by technological progress, that influenced the undergraduate curriculum, was the inception of software engineering (Cheetham *et al.*, 1988). The software crisis of the 1960s, marked by a meeting in Garmisch, Germany, in 1968, gave rise to the notion that the production of software should form an engineering discipline and this led to the development of courses of software engineering, although the movement was criticised as being a "bandwagon". Indeed, another conference on the history of software engineering, held in 1996 in Germany, concluded that software engineering had failed to become established. (Ceruzzi, 1998) Meanwhile, in the late 1980s, the concept of advanced courses in Information Systems Engineering (ISE) was gaining currency (Buckingham and Land, 1987) based on earlier models provided by the Association of Computing Machinery (ACM) and IFIP. An information system was defined as a human activity, which may or may not use computer systems, and the definition thus emphasised the system's socio-technical aspect, so that the training of an IS engineer would differ from that of a computer scientist.

Raymont (1986) of the National Computing Centre reported in 1986 on the then prominence of the debate about skills shortages in computing, including reports published by the Department of Trade and Industry, which had led to various educational initiatives. The Manpower Services Commission funded the Youth Training Scheme (YTS), which provided instruction in electronics and computing to school leavers in Information Technology Centres (ITeCs), the emphasis being on hands-on experience. (Griffiths, 1986) It also funded the Threshold Scheme, created in 1976, to train 17 – 19 year-olds to meet shortages for computing staff. The scheme, consisting of off-the-job training and work placements and operated almost entirely through further education colleges, handled about 1200 trainees annually. A parallel scheme was the Job Training Scheme, which the Manpower Services Commission funded from 1981; it included high level courses, run in higher education, in areas of "leading edge" technology, such as telecommunications, which annually handled about 400 trainees. A larger contingent, about 3500 annually took the basic entry-level skills training for the unemployed; trainees were selected on the basis of aptitude test and interview. Buckingham (1986) reported that a recent extension to the Youth Training Scheme as well as the new Certificate in Pre-Vocational Education (CPVE) and the Technical and Vocational Educational Initiative (TVEI) may provide a basis for development of careers in computing. CPVE was a one-year vocational course for 16 year-old school leavers. TVEI was a vocational curriculum for 14 – 18 year-olds.

Also providing input into the education of computing personnel during this period was the putative professional body for computing, the British Computer Society. Perkin (1996) advocated the notion of a professional, post-industrial society led by a wide range of experts, based on highly skilled human capital, which forms the main source of income-generating wealth. He described a professional ideal based on: trained and certified expertise out of the ordinary, selection by merit and by similarly trained experts, ascent through ability and education as well as mastery of a skilled service vital to fellow citizens (Perkin, 1989). According to Perkin's model, it is necessary for the professions to control the supply of specialised expertise into the labour market to safeguard their worth as a scarce resource and hence sustain the rewards, such as a secure income, enjoyed by their members. This protection would be through control of the market and exclusion of the unqualified. Closure occurs through restrictions on training and qualification, and acquisition of a state monopoly. (Perkin, 1989, p. 378) Perkin argued that the universities act as the "gatekeepers" to the professions (Perkin, 1989, p. 395). Between 1858 and 1960 all the large professions changed their training to the universities, instead of it being through apprenticeships and independent vocational courses. However, it behoved the professional bodies to maintain control, which they did through accrediting courses, offering exemption from professional exams and their academic members infiltrating the governing bodies of universities. Other models of the profession (Pavalko, 1971, p. 26; Moore, 1970) emphasise the importance of a long, specialised training period, with establishment of training facilities taking place during the process of professionalisation from an occupation to a profession (Millerson, 1964).

In the field of education, as well as creating, administering and reviewing its own system of professional examinations (Vickers, 1980; Ibbett, *et al.*, 1983; The Editor, 1983), the BCS, in the form of the Education Board, studied the qualifications to which members of the profession could aspire, and how appropriate they were. The Education Board was also interested in computing education in schools, international developments and the use of texts and training equipment (Bridger, 1968).

Actual input by the BCS into sub-degree courses, other than Higher National Diplomas offered by the polytechnics, appears to have been limited (Buckingham, 1981). The BCS was concerned, however, with education at degree level for the computing profession. From the inception of the BCS qualifying examination in the late 1960s the BCS accredited higher education courses. Until 1984 this was by means of simply examining the course documentation; from 1984 accreditation visits were carried out (Conway and Hooper, 1988). In 1981 the BCS proposed a Professional Development Scheme (PDS) for members in employment who wished to improve the standard of their work, particularly to assist their transition from Associate to full Member of the BCS (Sizer and Jackson, 1981). In 1986 Griffiths commented on the BCS PDS scheme and a government run equivalent which was in operation: the Computing Services Industry Training Council's Training and Career Development Programme. He believed that the latter encouraged a structured approach to in-company career planning, whereas he commended the PDS scheme, for its thorough determination of the relationship between different jobs in the computing area. (Griffiths, 1986)

3. CONCLUSIONS

In the field of education the BCS did a great deal of work in establishing the BCS professional examinations and a system of course accreditation at higher education level. It also created a Professional Development Scheme to improve the standard of workmanship of employees in the computing field. It reviewed and offered informed comment on all aspects of computer education, including sub-degree vocational awards, although these were managed by publicly funded bodies. However, it failed to achieve control of the training of computer professionals because employers were not bound to employ members of the BCS, and hence persons accredited by the BCS, for computer-related work. The British Government clearly influenced the content of courses at higher education and further education level, analysing and reporting on the projected staffing needs of the British computer industry, and creating bodies such as the Manpower Services Commissions to oversee government-funded developments such as the Threshold Scheme. Industry was involved in government or BCS-sponsored reviews, such as the 1970 Select Committee on Science and Technology. Industry was also the customer of the educational institutions, either directly, or indirectly, through its influence on potential students. Thus these three groups were responsible for moulding the content of courses in computing in Britain at degree and sub-degree level/technician level from the early 1960s to the late 1980s.

REFERENCES

Barritt, M.M., 1960, Computer courses for colleges. *The Computer Bulletin,* (Dec. 1960) pp. 82–83.

Barritt, M.M., 1962, Formal examinations for computer personnel. *The Computer Bulletin,* (Sept. 1962) pp. 55-56.

BCS (1970, National Diploma and Certificate courses. *The Computer Bulletin,* (Dec. 1970) p. 411.

Bell, R.T. and Robson, E.H., 1986, Some remarks on data processing degrees. *The Computer Bulletin,* (Dec. 1986) pp. 26-29.

Brandin, D.H. and Harrison, M., 1987, *The Technology War: A Case for Competitiveness.* New York; Chichester (etc.): John Wiley & Sons Inc., p.67.

Bridger, M., 1968, A background to the work of the Education Board. *The Computer Bulletin,* (June 1968) pp. 45 & 47.

Buckingham, R.A., 1967, Review of recent developments in computer education. *The Computer Bulletin,* (June 1967), pp. 6–10.

Buckingham, R.A., 1981, Education and training in computing. *The Computer Bulletin,* (June 1981) pp. 22–24.

Buckingham, R.A., 1986, The changing face of vocational education in computing. *The Computer Bulletin,* (June 1986) pp. 26, 27 & 29.

Buckingham, R.A. and Land, F.F., 1987, Education for ISE: what does it mean? *The Computer Bulletin,* (June 1987) pp. 33-35.

Campbell-Kelly, M., 1995, ICL and the evolution of the British mainframe. *The Computer Journal,* **38**(5), pp. 406-412.

Ceruzzi, P. E., 1998, A history of modern computing, 1st edition, Cambridge, Mass: MIT Press.

Cheetham, A.W., Knowles, P.J. and Woolliams, P.R., 1988, Software engineering: space invader of the 1980's? *The Computer Bulletin,* (Sept. 1988) pp. 24-25.

Colin, A., 1971, Universities and training. *The Computer Bulletin,* (July 1971) p. 246.

Conway, D. & Hooper, G., 1988, Accreditation of courses. *The Computer Bulletin,* (Sept. 1988, pp. 4, 5 & 7.

Cordata, J.W., 1997, Economic preconditions that made possible application of commercial computing in the United States. *IEEE Annals of the History of Computing,* **19**(3), pp. 27-39.

Day, C., 1974, The unsolved problem of computer science. *The Computer Bulletin,* (Sept. 1974) pp. 18-19.

Editor (1962, Computer comment: Committee on Higher Education (The Robbins Committee). *The Computer Bulletin,* (June 1962) pp. 2-3.

Gibson, R.P., 1964, Computer training facilities. *The Computer Bulletin,* (Mar. 1964) pp. 119-121.

Griffiths, J., 1986, Education and training for computing: an MSC perspective. *The Computer Bulletin,* (March 1986) pp. 4–6.

Hughson, I.S., 1964, Commercial computer education. *The Computer Bulletin,* (June 1964) pp. 13-16.

Ibbett, R.N., Cottam, I.D. & Zobel, R.N., 1983, Revisions to examination syllabuses. *The Computer Bulletin,* (Sept. 1983) pp. 5–7.

Joubert, G.R. and Stander, L.O., (1970, A new approach to the presentation of computer science courses. *The Computer Bulletin,* (Oct. 1970) pp. 342–343.

King, P.J.H., 1976, A taxonomy of computer science. *The Computer Bulletin,* (June 1976) pp. 28-30.

Land, F., 1975, Report on degrees in data processing. *The Computer Journal,* **18,** pp. 382–398.

Millerson, G., 1964, *The Qualifying Associations: A study in professionalization.* London: Routledge & Kegan Paul Ltd.

Moore, W.E., 1970, *The professions: roles and rules.* New York: Russell Sage Foundation.

Moreton, R., 1977, Computing courses in universities. *The Computer Bulletin,* (Mar. 1977) pp. 26,27 & 30.

Owen, G., 1999, *From Empire to Europe: The Decline and Revival of British Industry since the Second World War.* London: HarperCollins Publishers.

Pavalko, R.M., 1971, *Sociology of Occupations and Professions.* Itasca, Ill.: F.E. Peacock Publishers, Inc.

Penney, G., 1975, BCS proposals for a first degree in data processing. *The Computer Bulletin,* (Sept. 1975) pp. 4, 5 & 7.

Perkin, H., 1989, *The rise of professional society: England since 1880.* London; New York: Routledge.

Perkin, H., 1996, *The Third Revolution: Professional elites in the modern world.* London; New York: Routledge.

Raymont, P., 1986, Skills shortages and the user. *The Computer Bulletin,* (March 1986) pp. 2–3.

Samet, P.A., 1968, The education of DP managers. *The Computer Bulletin,* (Sept. 1968) pp. 190-191.

Simpson, D. and Kerridge, J., 1975, Part time education in computing. *The Computer Bulletin,* (Dec. 1975) pp. 24-25.

Sizer, T.R.H. & Jackson, B., 1981, Professional development programme. *The Computer Bulletin,* (Dec. 1981) pp. 5 & 14.

Staple, K. & Shaw, R., 1981, BEC/TEC awards in computer studies. *The Computer Bulletin,* (Dec. 1981) pp. 6–8.

Stevens, P.C., 1969, City and Guilds and computer education. *The Computer Bulletin,* (Mar. 1969) pp. 82–85.

Sviedrys, R., 1970, "The rise of physical science at Victorian Cambridge," in R. McCormmach (ed.), *Historical Studies in the Physical Sciences 2.* Philadelphia: University of Pennsylvania Press, pp. 127–151.

Vickers, T., 1980, The 1979 BCS Examination: conference report. *The Computer Bulletin,* (March 1980) pp. 22–23.

Wegner, P., 1963, The Hatfield Conference on Computer Education. *The Computer Bulletin,* (Sept. 1963) pp. 45-49.

IS IT LEGAL YET?

Social Issues in Computing and Teacher Education in Australia

Anthony J. Jones
The University of Melbourne, Australia
E-Mail: A.Jones@unimelb.edu.au

Abstract: The widespread application of computers throughout the daily life of most people has brought about changes in the things we do and how we do them. Schools in many countries now make use of computer-based learning technologies at all levels of education, from kindergarten through secondary schooling to tertiary education. Use of computers for teaching and learning cannot be separated from effects that computerization has had on education and the wider community. Values, ethics and social issues related to computing represent one significant area of study for teachers and students. The purpose of this paper is to review the place given to computer related values, ethics and social issues in schools and teacher education.

Key words: Values; Ethics; Social issues; Teacher education

1. INTRODUCTION

When computers began to be used for teaching and learning in schools and universities there was little commercial educational software for sale. Teachers often used one of the small number of programming languages available to write, test and use educational software with their own students. Because those teachers who introduced computing into schools and developed their own software were enthusiasts, they met and corresponded with like-minded teachers. Inevitably this led to software being exchanged, and this was probably the origin of a software swapping culture that quickly developed in schools. Not only did a culture of software swapping develop among these computer-enthusiast teachers, it flourished and continued to exist for decades.

What is the situation now? Articles about computer related ethics, values and social issues in mass circulation newspapers is one clue to community awareness of these matters. In September 2003 a daily Melbourne (Australia) newspaper published the four articles listed in Table 1.

Table 1. Sample of social issues articles from The Age newspaper

A week before it opened in US cinemas, a copy of the film *The Hulk* was available on illicit file-sharing networks. (Piracy, 2003)
The Australian government has introduced into parliament proposed anti-spam legislation that will penalize those convicted of illicitly spreading mass unsolicited electronic material up to AU$1.1 million per day.(Cochrane, 2003)
Technology, like gambling and heroin, is addictive. We're driven or forced into buying new gadgets and constantly upgrading our technology. (Forno, 2003. p.6)
.. if online learning is becoming a method of semi-automated teaching, it could be big business. In Britain, e-learning already is. ... The British are driving e-learning into their schools by creating demand. (Wilson, 2003, p.10)

At first glance there might appear no obvious links between these articles, however there are at least two significant connecting factors. First, each article relates to an issue associated with the use (and misuse) of computers and computing applications. A second, and perhaps more worrying, connection between the articles is that they were all published in a single issue of the daily newspaper, albeit in a weekly IT supplement.

In addition to the four articles referred to above, the same edition of the IT supplement also contained an article on copyright and intellectual property, a book review about corporate IT security, and another on computer espionage, a case study of an Australian bank's approach to offshore outsourcing in order to reduce costs, an article on collaboration between Australian and US bodies responsible for emergency response to hacking, as well as an article detailing how dependent most people in developed countries are on computers for work, recreation, and at home. Each of these items also relates to computerization and associated implications for society.

This paper explores some of what has occurred between the swapping of software by pioneers of educational computing and the apparent high level of computer-related crime and associated issues in 2003. The theme that is explored concerns how ethics, values and social issues of computing have been incorporated or ignored in school and teacher education curricula.

2. IN THE BEGINNING

Norbert Wiener was probably the first person to write extensively on computers and ethics (Bynum, 2000). Long before computers were artifacts of everyday life Wiener was thinking and writing about the potential ethical and social issues arising from a range of newly developing technologies, including computerization (Wiener 1948, 1954).

In 1968 this author was teaching mathematics in a secondary school for boys. On an experimental basis he was permitted to introduce some computer programming to a class of high achievers. Possibly because it was part of mathematics, or possibly because he knew no better, the focus was entirely on learning the FORTRAN programming language to extend the mathematical experiences of the students. There is no record of any mention of computer-related values, ethics or social issues. The same remained true until the mid 1970s as the author continued to teach at a secondary school as well as teaching a computing subject to pre-service primary teachers.

Even before desktop computers appeared in large numbers in schools, teachers were teaching about possible ethical and social issues resulting from the newly developing computer technology. As early as 1982 articles about values and social issues were appearing in newly established computing journals for teachers (Finkel, 1983; Letellier, 1982). In a 1992 article in *The Computing Teacher* it was noted that "Teachers have told students about computer ethics for years" (Weller et al., 1992 p.20). The authors then referred to a series of articles from a 1984 issue of the same journal. These articles had titles such as "Ethics and computer use" (Gilliland & Pollard, 1984), "A question of ethics" (Hannah & Matus, 1984) and "Computers, kids and values" (Taffee, 1984).

It is impossible to accurately quantify the growth of publications that address some part of computer interrelated values, ethics or social issues. However there is no doubt these areas have become more significant and more widely publicized as computer use has spread throughout society. As a very simplistic measure, Table 2 lists the number of publications found in the ERIC database using search parameters ***(computer) AND (ethics)***. The number of publications decreases dramatically when the terms **(education) OR (school)** are added to the search parameters.

Table 2. "Computer ethics" publications listed in the ERIC database.

Years	Number of items found	Cumulative total
1966[4] - 1969	8	8
1970 – 1979	45	53
1980 – 1989	229	282
1990 – 1999	460	742
2000 - 2003[5]	126	868

[4] Beginning of ERIC electronic records.
[5] Searches conducted on 14 January 2004 at http://www.eduref.org.

No matter what approach is used to analyze these data, it is evident that that very little has been published in this area. As noted above, when the search is limited to publications specifically about *computer ethics* and *schools* the number of publications is halved. A perusal of titles of remaining publications shows that many concern ethics for administrators or counselors and do not relate to classroom practice.

3. PRACTICAL SOLUTIONS

Faculties of education, school curriculum developers, ICT textbook authors, and ICT teachers do not collectively appear to give values and social issues relating to ICT a sufficient level of prominence. There are some curriculum references to values and social issues in school curricula, but often only at senior secondary levels rather than throughout all the levels of education and schooling in which students use or learn about ICT. As soon as primary school students begin to access electronic encyclopedias and the World Wide Web in their search for information for projects, they confront issues relating to intellectual property, copyright, acknowledgment and plagiarism. It would appear that by default many schools allow students to break laws relating to all of the above. In general this happens because teachers and parents focus on using technology and not the associated responsibilities and implications.

The case for students and teachers knowing about social and ethical issues associated with ICT throughout all subject areas of schooling might not appear as obvious or as strong as for learning about them in ICT specific subjects. However it can be argued that that it is vitally important for all students, not just those who study ICT, to have well developed understandings of ethical and legal issues relating to ICT use. It appears there is little evidence of this actually occurring on a consistent basis in primary and secondary schools. Some of the reasons for this are probably the same as those outlined above in relation to specialist ICT subjects and teachers. However a major cause is the over-emphasis on what *can* be done with technology and a corresponding lack of coverage of the *consequences* of doing things with technology. Often teachers and texts focus on the quite dramatic and valuable changes that can result from increased use of technology without giving sufficient consideration to the social, legal and ethical implications of these developments.

By the early 1980s articles were appearing in computing journals for teachers with titles such as "Crime in the classroom?" (Letellier, 1982) and "When is a pirate a thief?" (Finkel, 1983). Teachers were being informed of some of the ethical and legal issues relating to computing through journals and professional associations. However the quantity of articles published through the 1980s and well into the 1990s warning about the ramifications of copying software and other illegal and un-ethical practices suggest that it was a widespread problem in schools.

As school computing curricula became formalized, aspects of values, ethics and social issues were taught more consistently and in more organized ways. Related topics also became more prominent in textbooks. In Victoria, the first formal curriculum for a school computing subject was developed in the late 1970s and included "social implications" as one of the four areas of study. The most popular textbook for this subject (Woodhouse at al., 1982) included a chapter that introduced students to some of the ethical and social issues related to the technology of the time. It appears certain that one of the authors was approached to contribute to this book on the basis of personal interest and knowledge of computer-related social implications.

Teacher education has been slower than schools to accept the importance of computer related values, ethics and social issues. Until the mid 1990s, Australian pre-service teacher education courses were not required to include computing subjects. Then major credentialing authorities and employers demanded that every new teacher possess a range of computing skills and be aware of major technology related ethical and social issues.

In a pre-service subject for secondary IT teachers currently offered at The University of Melbourne, students undertake several projects and assessment tasks that involve them learning about social and ethical issues. One complicating factor is that many of the most appropriate techniques for teaching social and ethical issues at school level are based around strategies most employed by teachers of English and social studies, rather than teachers in the sciences or IT. Effective strategies include discussions and debates, role plays, research using a variety of sociological sources, essay writing, and a consideration of emotions and feelings. The majority of IT teachers have a background in science or business studies, and they find using such strategies to teach social and ethical issues more difficult than the technical aspects of their subjects.

For other secondary teachers in training, and for prospective elementary teachers, being able to apply humanities-based teaching strategies is less of a problem. Because they are not going to be specialized ICT teachers they rarely come into contact with concepts of technology related ethics, values, and social issues being classroom topics that should concern them. Far too many teachers who use ICT with students, but are not ICT teachers, never raise technology-related legal and ethical issues with students, even though schools throughout the world appear to have acceptable use policies that students and their parents are required to agree to and sign.

However school acceptable use policies have failed to go far enough. Usually they are little more than an attempt to safeguard a school from legal charges that might arise from students who infringe copyright or ethical statutes while using school computers. Rarely is there an education program for students and parents that complements the signing of an acceptable use agreement. For classroom teachers the major problem relates to students plagiarizing material from an electronic resource and failing to acknowledge the source and ownership of ideas and images that are used in assignments.

The National Educational Technology Standards project (NETS, 2002) includes ideas for including "analyzing legal, moral, and ethical dilemmas" within teacher education. Not only are these issues raised with at these levels, but quite specific activities and roles are designated for teacher educators and the beginning teachers. Although it might appear elsewhere, a major weakness of this section is that the vignettes used focus on out-of-classroom situations. While this is understandable because the section is about professional preparation, there is no link to classroom teaching about the legal, moral and ethical dilemmas students encounter in their daily lives.

Similar comments apply to the "ICT skills test" (TTA, 2003) all teachers in-training in England must pass before they gain accreditation to teach. This test aims to guarantee that new teachers have an appropriate grounding in basic ICT skills. Again, as with the NETS material, there is no statement informing new teachers that it is the duty of every teacher to be aware of, to uphold personally and professionally, and to ensure that students do not breach laws concerning legal, moral and ethical issues relating to all educational technologies, and to computing in particular.

4. CONCLUSION

When computers were rare in commerce and industry, and did not exist in schools, what little educational interest there was focused on the potential of computers for relieving humans of mundane, difficult, or dangerous tasks. Most people did not know what computers were doing, because much of it was related to military applications and was restricted. It was only when computers became smaller, simpler and generally available that they became associated with crime and social issues such as privacy and replacing people in employment. Today teachers and students use computer technology as a normal part of the education process, and there is an obvious need to know about the effects of technology as well as the applications.

REFERENCES

Bynum, T., 2000, *A very short history of computer ethics.* (September 17, 2003); http://apa.udel.edu/publications/newsletters/v99n2/computs/index.asp.

Bynum, T., 2001, Computer Ethics: Basic Concepts and Historical Overview, in: *The Stanford Encyclopedia of Philosophy,* E. Zalta, ed., (September 17, 2003); http://plato.stanford.edu/archives/win2001/entries/ethics-computer/.

Cochrane, N., 2003, Government hopes to send message with anti-spam bill. *The Age,* 23 September. Next, p. 3.

Finkel, L., 1983, When is a pirate a thief? *Electronic Learning,* **3**(2):26-28.

Forno, R., 2003, Hooked on high-tech. *The Age,* 23 September. Next, p. 6.

Gilliland, K. & Pollard, M., 1984, Ethics and computer use. *The Computing Teacher,* **12**(1): 19-23.

Hannah, L. & Matus, C., 1984, A question of ethics. *The Computing Teacher,* **12**(1):11-14.

Letellier, L., 1982, Crime in the classroom? *Electronic Learning,* **1**(3):42-44, 51.

Marsh, M., 1998, *Piracy, pornography, plagiarism, propaganda, privacy: Teaching children to be responsible users of technology.* (September 17, 2003); http://www.computerlearning.org/articles/Ethics98.htm.

NETS, 2002, *Analyzing legal, moral and ethical dilemmas.* (February 14, 2004): http://cnets.iste.org/teachers/.

Piracy, 2003, Piracy becoming a monster of a problem. *The Age,* September 23. Next, p. 3.

Taffee, S., 1984, Computers, kids and values. *The Computing Teacher,* **12**(1):15-18.

TTA, 2003, *ICT skills test.* Teacher Training Agency. (February 14, 2004): http://www.tta.gov.uk/.

Weller, H., Repman, J., Rooze, G. & Parker, R., 1992, Students and computer ethics: An alternative to preaching. *The Computing Teacher,* **20**(1): 20-22.

Wiener, N., 1948, *Cybernetics: or Control and Communication in the Animal and the Machine.* Technology Press: Cambridge, MA.

Wiener, N., 1954, *The Human Use of Human Beings: Cybernetics and Society.* 2nd ed., Doubleday: New York.

Wilson, E., 2003, Music e-learning sounds a positive note for online hopes. *The Age,* September 23. p.10.

Woodhouse, D., Johnstone, G., & McDougall, A., 1982, *Computer Science.* John Wiley & Sons: Brisbane.

THE EVOLUTION OF E-INCLUSION

Technology in Education for the Vision Impaired

Scott Hollier and Iain Murray
Curtin University of Technology, Western Australia
E-mail: info@scotthollier.com; i.murray@ece.curtin.edu.au

Abstract: The 1970s and 1980s saw a rapid take-up in the use of personal computers. During the same time period, society began to move towards providing equity for people with disabilities. As legislators around the world created new disability and Information Technology policies, more people with disabilities were given access to education and the evolving computing tools provided unprecedented educational opportunities. These opportunities were due to the use of new technologies such as outputting of electronic text to voice synthesizers. The provision of assistive technology was not only helpful; it also provided education through a medium that was previously unavailable, particular to the blind and vision impaired. For much of the 1980s the development of text-processing sensory technologies, connected to personal computers, led to a closer equality between the educational services of the able-bodied and people with disabilities.

Unfortunately this evolution as not without notable difficulties: issues surrounding the cost of products, the lack of support from large corporations and choice of platform resulted in substantial difficulties for educators in the assessment of appropriate technology. In addition, many of these products became largely redundant in the late-1980s as corporations began to place more emphasis on the Graphical User Interface (GUI). Although the GUI was remarkably successful in allowing the general public to gain better access to personal computing, it's non-text nature once again caused a digital divide for people with disabilities. Although it is clear that the evolution of the personal computer has had a significant impact on the provision of education for people with disabilities, this paper highlights the historical repetition where innovation is prioritized above e-inclusion.

Key words: Vision Impairment; Education; Disability; Computing history; E-inclusion; Digital divide

1. INTRODUCTION

The History of Computing in relation to education contains a vast array of achievements. Few would argue that the framework established in the development of personal computing in the 1970s and 1980s essentially changed the way we interact as a global community.

Although it is important to reward such profound and revolutionary achievements, it is easy to forget that during this time period there are interesting developmental parallels in relation to human rights and social justice. In regards to people with disabilities, the evolution of technology is not just an achievement, but also an opportunity to gain unprecedented access to products and services unlike any other time in history. This e-inclusive evolution also, in turn, provided the tools necessary to move beyond individual education and establish the education of our society in the importance of equity in all areas of daily life.

In relation to people with disabilities, the benefits of the new electronic medium were clear: as approximately 80% of our traditional education structure is presented in a visual format, students with vision impairment were unable to access information that is common to other students until the personal computer provided the opportunity to translate text into other mediums, such as voice. (Levtzion-Korach et al, 2000, Ross, et al, 2001)

Yet despite the promise of unprecedented educational opportunities, the rapid change in technological growth often left people with disabilities in the wake of innovation. As a result, people with disabilities were given a taste of substantially empowering technology, only to be denied those opportunities in the ever-growing desire to move forward. Although computing achievements are often seen as a double-edged sword for people with disabilities, the evolution of e-inclusion has provided unprecedented support to the creation of education of the individual and education of our society.

2. THE ADVENT OF PERSONAL COMPUTING

The dawn of mainstream computing in the mid- to late-1970s provided an opportunity for society to increase their productivity and entertainment needs within the home and the workplace. The speed of growth and the battle for supremacy between computer offerings from companies such as Commodore, Apple, Radio Shack and Atari led one commentator to reflect on this time as "...one of the most remarkable phenomena of recent history." (Davies, 1984, p. i) As people discovered the benefits of home computing, Western governments were presented with a difficult challenge in creating legislation to meet the emerging legal issues that had appeared as a result of such technology.

2.1 Equity and Technology

During the same time period, another rapid change was taking place in our society: the evolution of equity and social justice. Until the mid-1970s, the rights of people with disabilities were very limited. In order to raise awareness and provide some legislative framework for government policy, the World Health Organisation (WHO) released official definitions for the terms disability, impairment, and handicap. It also show-cased some of the prototype accessible technology during the International Year of Disabled Persons. (Richards, 1982) One of the more significant items on display at this time was the SYNTE2, one of the first microprocessor-based and portable speech synthesizers in the world.

The establishment of official definitions of disability led to the development of disability policy through the early to mid-1980s. The development of these policies led to a refinement of disability terminology and an increased societal acceptance of people with disabilities as equals. One of the most significant changes in disability policy resulted in increased access to education. Countries such as the United States, England and Australia had notable increases of disabled students in tertiary institutions in the late-1970s and through the 1980s due directly to various public laws in the US and equivalent policies, such as the Disability Services Act of 1986 in Australia (Clear, 2000) Not only were enrollments increasing but the proportion of people with disabilities who completed tertiary education in the same time period increased as well.

3. ASSISTIVE TECHNOLOGY

Although the framework of disability legislation is certainly a major factor for the improvements in education for people with disabilities during the late-1970s and 1980s, the parallel development of computing technology also played a significant role in providing additional educational opportunities for people with disabilities. One of the biggest benefits of having data in electronic format was the ability to easily output data in an accessible format. Many of the early assistive technologies focused on assisting people who were blind or had vision impairment via such popular speech synthesizers based on the Votrax speech synthesis chip. Examples of these synthesizers included the Brother Caiku, Eke, Humanica and Task. (Lemmetty, 2004) Over the course of the 1980s, other products were made to assist people with different types of disunities through the use of light pens for people with mobility impairments, and on-screen alerts for people with hearing impairments.

Although the increased individual opportunities were indeed beneficial, the development process of technology for people with disabilities was not progressing as rapidly as the growth of the Information Technology industry: With the exception of IBM, few mainstream computing firms seemed to take issues of accessibility seriously, and it became apparent in the mid-1980s that in order for education to benefit from the computing revolution, it would require a major shift in public education practices to truly highlight the needs of people with disabilities in the development of Information Technology. (Lansdown, 1980)

As a result, most of the development of assistive technology was undertaken by specialist companies that unfortunately resulted in assistive technology becoming expensive and often out of the price range of those that needed it. This left both educators and legislators with dilemmas regarding which equipment provided the best platform for the development of assistive technology. Little attention was given to the incorporation of emerging technology for people with disabilities by legislators; this was due in part to the difficulties in meeting the legislative needs of mainstream technology and in part because of the difficulty in providing broad guidelines that could encompass all the competing 8-bit and 16-bit computing platforms in the market. The fear in disability circles was that this lack of action would result in severe computer inequity, leading one of the more disadvantaged sections of our society to become alienated from a world that was becoming increasingly technologically dependent. (Gergen, 1986)

In relation to the specific struggle of people with disabilities in education, there were additional difficulties in both affording and providing assistive technologies. With no mandate from government policy, it was left to the educational institutions to determine the best technological needs for their students. The benefits of assistive technology were rapidly becoming apparent, but the small client base made it difficult to justify the costs involved. The choice of platform also had to be determined:

For example, the Epson HX-20 was determined by many Australian educators to be a vital tool for developers in the early to mid-1980s for blind and vision impaired people. The reason for this selection was due to it's portability, built-in screen, and relative affordability at approximately $4,000AU$. However, software speech synthesis could be better handled by popular 8-bit machines such as the Commodore 64 and, in the mid- to late-1980s, the Commodore Amiga range of computers. Furthermore computers such as these also had support for light pen technology that would assist people with mobility issues. Furthermore, machines such as the Apple II were cheaper and already had a significantly larger user base that the Epson HX-20. (Gergen, 1986)

Figure 1. The Epson HX-20 microcomputer

4. EDUCATIONAL NEED

As the general public became more informed about the needs of people with disabilities, the wave of social change led to educators creating methods of assessment to provide accessible technology to people with disabilities in order to assist their educational needs. This was not just limited to the educational institution: it quickly became apparent that having a personal computer in the home would greatly assist in performing related tasks and the teaching of life skills. One such action plan determined that the most important elements of developments were based on the issues of the type of technology best suited to the user, the quality of technology, in what context would the technology be used, and what were it's primary strengths and weaknesses. These criteria, established in the 1980s, are still relevant today. (Bryant & Bryant, 2003)

Sometimes, however, the best intentions can often result in increased complexity within the selection process. Many educators have adopted Semelfort's guidelines (as cited in Bryant & Bryant), based again on the assessment process in the 1980s. Those guides include the need to assemble a technology evaluation team including teachers, students and appropriate professionals, the consideration of input from the user, the focus on the functionality of the selected technology, the need for simplicity and benefits of the product. Although these guidelines may appear to be a sensible and thoughtful approach to the provision of accessible technology, the time required to select a number of professions, make the assessments and gain a full understanding of the user requires a significant amount of time and often resulted in students with a disability floundering behind fellow classmates due to these unfortunate delays. (Dorman, 1998)

5. STANDARDISATION OF PERSONAL COMPUTING

Fortunately the progression of the mid- to late-1980s revealed many benefits for people with disabilities. As the existing technology became more established, the price of assistive technology came down. The development of assistive technology became centralized to the IBM PC platform due to it's increasingly popularity with business and educational institutions that embraced this platform to ensure educational training resulting in a knowledge of IT products in the workforce. The other advantage of the IBM PC was that the material was all text-based, assistive technologies such as speech synthesizers had been refined to a point where they could easily interpret the information. (Lemmetty, 2004)

At the close of the 1980s people with disabilities were getting unprecedented access to information. The legislators were also starting to focus more on disability policy, with the United States in particular working on the strengthening of its disability laws. Although the evolution of technology was still seemed to be a little volatile for specific IT-based legislation for people with disabilities, the ongoing public education of the needs of people with disabilities gained significant strength during this time. (Bricout, 2001)

Although text-based computing was now in prominence, the end of the 1980s revealed a computing spectre that was gaining in popularity, the Graphical User Interface (GUI). Gaining significant popularity from the commercial success of the Apple Macintosh released in 1984 (Sanford, 2004), numerous platforms began to focus on GUI implementation. 16-bit systems such as the Commodore Amiga and the Atari ST were developed as GUI operating platforms. Even older 8-bit platforms such as the Commodore 64 received a GUI overhaul from programs such as GEOS being built into the sale of 8-bit machines. The fading CP/M operating system and the popular MS-DOS operating system were now making way for new developed by Microsoft and IBM on the IBM PC platform. (Necasek, 2004)

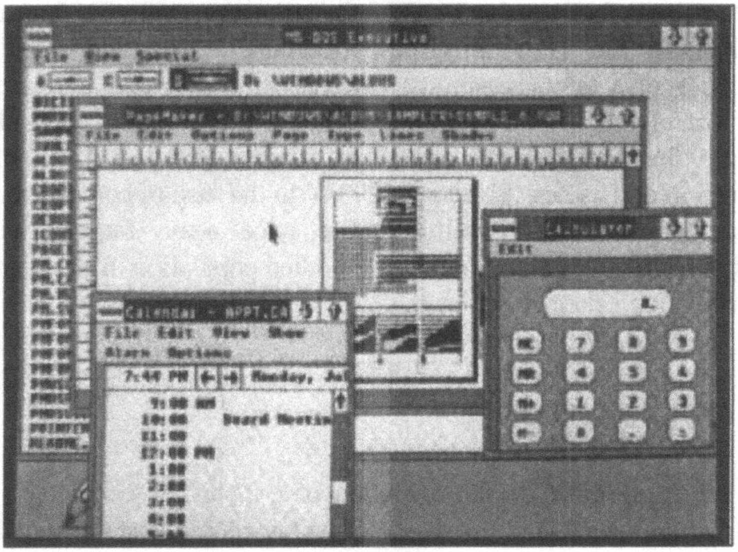

Figure 2. Microsoft Windows 2.0

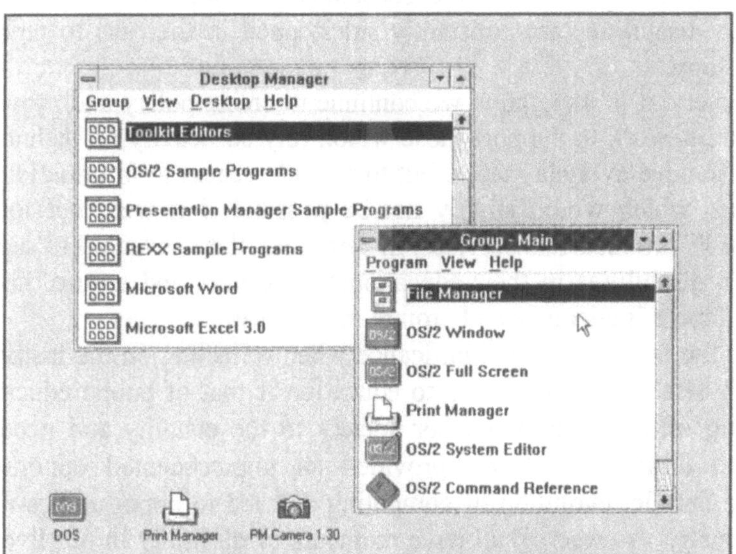

Figure 3. IBMs OS/2 version 1.1

The twilight of the 1980s saw two GUI products gaining popularity for the PC platform: Microsoft Windows 2.0 and IBM's OS/2 1.1. Although both products still had text-based DOS functionality, software developers were embracing the GUI interfaces. (Lessard, 2004) Although IBM endeavored to provide accessibility features in OS/2 with a degree of success, most of the large corporations did not implemented accessibility features into the new interface which rendered which left much of the assistive technology useless. (Necasek, 2004) In the rush of competition and innovation, people with disabilities were once again faced with the likelihood of trying to catch up to the able-bodied population in an attempt to embrace technological equality.

6. CONCLUSION

When reflecting back on the evolution of e-inclusive technology, it is easy to forget that "each and every one of us knows moments of inability." (Shearer, 1981, p. 2) Although access to technology for people with disabilities has improved considerably since it's initial chaotic inception, the pattern of innovation, division, and e-inclusion is a constantly repeating one: from the dawn of home computing through the introduction of the GUI and more recently the Internet, we are constantly reminded that the needs of people with disabilities are constantly sidestepped in the rush to embrace new technology.

As a society, it is imperative we continue to create policy and provide a corporate framework to support those which rely so heavily on technology not just to achieve everyday tasks, but to provide access to information and opportunities which would simply not be possible if it were not for the availably of IT products and services. In particular, there is a need to support people with disabilities in their educational endeavors and ensure that the provision of tools is adequate and prompt in delivery.

Perhaps the issue of most significance when reflecting on the history of people with disabilities in relation to education is that of public education. The ongoing effort to enlighten our society to the equality and needs of people with disabilities clearly provided an unprecedented opportunity through the parallel evolution of computing and led to opportunities never seen previously. As we will all have moments of disability in our lives, to help people with disabilities will in turn assist all those in the community. Through individual and public education, the evolution of e-inclusion will continue to flourish and provide equal computing products and services to all.

REFERENCES

Bricout, J. C., 2001, Making computer-mediated education responsive to the accommodation needs of students with disabilities. *Journal of Social Work Education, 37*(2), 267.

Bryant, D., & Bryant, B., 2003, *Assistive Technology for People with Disabilities*. Boston: Pearson Education.

Clear, M., 2000, *Promises, promises: disability and terms of inclusion*. Leichhardt: Federation Press.

Davies, A. C., 1984, The Home Computer Course Introduction. *The Home Computer Course, 1*, i-ii.

Dorman, S., 1998, Assistive Technology benefits for students with disabilities. *Journal of School Health, 68*(3), 120-123.

Gergen, M., 1986, *Computer Technology for the Handicapped*. Minnesota: Crow River Press.

Kelley, P., Sanspree, M., and Davidson, R., 2000): Vision impairment in children and youth. In The lighthouse handbook of vision impairment and vision rehabilitation. 2:1111-1128. HOROWITZ (ed), Oxford University Press, New York.

Lansdown, R., 1980, *More Than Sympathy*. London: Tavistock Publications.

Lemmetty, S., 2004, *History and Development of Speech Synthesis*. Retrieved 11 Feb, 2004, from http://www.acoustics.hut.fi/~slemmett/dippa/chap2.html

Lessard, D., 2004, *PC Museum: History of Windows*. Retrieved 11 Feb, 2004, from http://members.fortunecity.com/pcmuseum/windows.htm

Levtzion-Korach, O., Tennenbaum, A., Schnitzen, R., and Ornoy, A. (2000): Early motor development of blind children. Journal of Paediatric and Child Health, 36:226-229.

Necasek, M., 2004, *The History of OS/2*. Retrieved 11 Feb, 2004, from http://pages.prodigy.net/michaln/history/timeline.html

Richards, J., 1982, *Towards Prevention of Permanent Disability in Australia*. Canberra: Australian Government Publishing Services.

Ross, G., Lipper, E., Abramson, D. and Preiser, L. (2001): The development of young children with retinoblastoma. *Archives of Pediatrics & Adolescent Medicine,* 155(1):80-83.

Sanford, G., 2004, *AppleHistory.com*. Retrieved 11 Feb, 2004, from http://www.apple-history.com/frames/?

Shearer, A., 1981, *Disability: Whose Handicap?* Oxford: Basil Blackwell Publishers.

ON THE ERA OF EDUCATIONAL HYPERMEDIA COMPUTING

From Simple Links to More Complex Structures

Anneli Heimbürger and Jari Multisilta
Tampere University of Technology, Finland
E-mail: anneli.heimburger@tut.fi; jari.multisilta@tut.fi

Abstract: The paper presents a timeline of information and communication technologies in learning since the days of Vannebar Bush's Memex, Douglas Engelbart's Augment, Ted Nelson's Xanadu, and PLATO systems to the current lively research and development work going on between the traditional hypertext research community and the World Wide Web Consortium (W3C). Hypermedia has been widely applied in computer assisted instruction and learning. Engelbart's NLS/Augment can be regarded as the first CSCW (Computer Supported Collaborative Work) environment. Later, such systems as Intermedia, Microcosm and Hypercard have successfully presented the ideas of hypertext in learning contexts. In this paper we discuss the development of learning theories and hypertext linking environments and their roles in today's networked and mobile learning environments.

Keywords: Information and communication technologies; ICT; Computer assisted instruction; CAI; Computer assisted learning; CAL; Hypertext linking; History; Future trends

1. INTRODUCTION

"The human mind operates by association. With one item in its grasp, it snaps instantly to the next that is suggested by the association of thoughts, in accordance with some intricate web trails carried by the cells of the brain, … the speed of action, the intricacy of trails, the detail of mental pictures, are awe-inspiring beyond all else in nature. Man cannot hopefully to duplicate this mental process artificially, but he certainly ought to be able to learn from it." (Bush, 1945)

Hypermedia integrates digital computing with the natural tendency of the human mind to think associatively and to manage information hierarchically. Hypermedia applications allow users to navigate collections of compound documents non-sequentially by (a) jumping backward and forward, (b) presenting an overview of the whole hyperdocument space to a user, (c) zooming in for details, (d) experiencing sequences of animation, sound or digital video, (e) reading the information at their own rate independent of place and time, and (f) learning by associations. Several research results have been published, which indicate that hypertext learning environments support interactive learning models (Burch, 2001; Crestani and Ntioudis, 2002; Harley, 2001; Hede, 2002; Mullier et al., 2002; Ohl, 2001; Oliver and McLoughlin, 2001).

Current network and mobile technologies together with World Wide Web course tools provide us with possibilities to build more and more challenging learning environments (Carlson and Repman, 2002). Even the differences between formal learning, informal learning and way of working are diminishing. Contextual access is predicted to be one of the most relevant means of retrieving information from the traditional and mobile Web; a user, a location, a device, and time determining the context.

Could it be that we, in our great enthusiasm for developing new technologies, have overlooked some pertinent pieces of knowledge which already were there before the Web: learning theories with best practices from classrooms and versatile hypertext links supporting associative thinking of human mind?

The remainder of the paper is organised as follows. A timeline of information and communication technologies in learning is presented in Section 2. The development of learning theories is discussed in Section 3. Development trends of hypertext linking are described in Section 4. Section 5 is reserved for conclusions.

2. TIMELINE OF INFORMATION AND COMMUNICATION TECHNOLOGIES IN LEARNING

Information and communication technologies (ICT) in learning, for example computer assisted instruction (CAI), computer aided learning (CAL) and hypermedia, have developed hand in hand with technological progress in computer science and information systems. In historical timeline of these technologies, five generations of mainstream computing environments can be identified (Table 1):

Table 1. Timeline of ICT in learning.

Year	Event
1st Generation: Time of microfiches and mainframes	
1945	Vannevar Bush proposed the Memex system, a microfiche-based system of documents and links, in his article entitled "As we may think". Memex foreshadowed the advent of hypertext. Fast access of information, ability to annotate, ability to link and to store trails of links were some requirements for the Memex specified by Bush. (Bush, 1945)
1960s	Several CAI projects started. Stanford project and the Programmed Learning and Teaching Operation (PLATO) system were influential CAI projects with heavy emphasis on educational research (Nievergelt, 1980; Pantages, 1976).
1962	Douglas Engelbart published a paper "Augmenting human intellect: A conceptual framework". Engelbart defined the functions necessary for computers to augment human abilities such as links between texts, electronic mail, screens with multiple windows, and facilities for collaborative work. Engelbart invented the mouse, outliner and idea processor, and on-line help systems integrated with software. Engelbart's NLS/Augment can be regarded as the first environment for Computer Supported Collaborative Work (CSCW). (Engelbart, 1963)
1965	Theodor Holm Nelson invented the term "hypertext" and presented it to the world. Ever since Nelson has continued his mission in life as universally acknowledged ideologist of hypertext. Xanadu and ZigZag are the two hypertext engines designed by Ted Nelson. (Nelson, 1987; Nelson, 2004)
1968-1988	Andries Van Dam and his team at Brown University (USA) developed the Hypertext Editing System and its extension File Retrieval and Editing Systems (FRESS). According to Van Dam, FRESS was the first system to have an undo function. The third and, nowadays the very classic, hypertext system developed by Van Dam and his group was called

Intermedia. Intermedia-based applications were used in teaching and learning biology and English literature at Brown University. Professors prepared their lessons and course materials and students created their reports. One of the remarkable ideas of Van Dam was the "web", a set of links that belongs together. This makes it possible for different users to create sets of links of their own on the same document. In present hypertext terminology these sets of links are called linkbases. (Berk & Devlin, 1991; Yankelovich et al., 1985; Van Dam, 1988)

1970s Mitre Corporation has a large-scale CAI project, Ticcit, for production of courseware on an industrial basis. Problem solving environments such as the Logo project and Smalltalk system have influenced many people. (Nievergelt, 1980)

2nd Generation: Time of workstations

1972-1983 According to Frank Halasz, ZOG, developed at Carnegie-Mellon University was the last first generation hypertext systems, which all run on mainframes. The second generation of hypertext authoring products, such as Intermedia and KMS, was born in the beginning of 1980s with the development of workstations. Faster computers, displays and networks supported more versatile user interfaces and collaborative work, for example within designers and engineers sharing the same KMS-based applications like technical documents on a computer network. (Berk & Devlin, 1991)

3rd Generation: Time of personal computers began

1985 Peter Brown invented Guide, the first commercial hypertext authoring system for personal computers. Guide was first available for Apple MacIntosh and in 1987 for IBM PC. There was less functionality than in mainframe and workstation-based products but graphical user interface and the possibility for link typing were new features.

1986 Xerox Palo Alto Research Center released NoteCards. NoteCards, KMS and Intermedia supported graphics and animation nodes. They also supported creation of graphical overviews of the structure of the hyperdocument. The overviews made it easier for users to navigate and decreased the cognitive overload followed by the "lost in hyperspace" phenomenon. (Halasz, 1988)

1986 ISO published the Standard Generalized Markup Language (SGML) which is the very basis for structured document and link management in today's Web (ISO 8879).

1987 HyperCard for Apple Macintosh was released. The metaphor of HyperCard is based on cards which form stacks. Cards are linked to other cards with link anchors called buttons. The IBM PC version of Hyperties developed at University of Maryland was introduced. Hyperties used the metaphor of an electronic book or encyclopaedia.

1989 Tim Berners-Lee proposed a distributed hypertext system for the management of general information at CERN (Berners-Lee, 1999).

1990s Usability of hypermedia systems began to be a serious matter of interest. Many usability laboratories were established around the world. Jacob Nielsen has published books under the titles Usability engineering and later Designing Web usability (Nielsen, 1993; Nielsen, 2000).

4th Generation: Era of the World Wide Web (WWW) started

1990 In November Tim Berners-Lee has programmed a point-and-click browser/editor that he called WorldWideWeb. On Christmas Day 1990 WorldWideWeb browser/editor was working on Berners-Lee's and his colleague Robert Cailliau's machines, communicating over Internet with the info.cern.ch –server. (Berners-Lee, 1999)

1993 In February, NCSA made the first version of Mosaic browser available over the Web (Berners-Lee, 1999).

1994 In April, Netscape released the commercialized version of the Mosaic (Berners-Lee, 1999).

1996 Microsoft's Internet Explorer was released (Berners-Lee, 1999).

1995- Open hypermedia research community indicated that the solution to many hypertext link management issues is to separate links from content. Several open hypermedia systems were implemented. Chimera, Hyper-G and Microcosm are examples of the classics, where support for non-embedded links inside and between WWW pages has been developed (Carr et al., 1995; Grønbæk and Trigg, 1999).

1996 Jari Multisilta at Tampere University of Technology has designed, implemented and evaluated a Hypermedia based Learning Environment (HMLE) for mathematics. Automatic link generation is one example of the HMLE's advanced functionalities. HMLE based Matrix Algebra I was one of the first complete courses implemented in World Wide Web. (Multisilta, 1996)

1997 ISO published a standard Hypermedia/Time-based Structuring Language (HyTime) (ISO/IEC 10744). HyTime as such was too complicated and abstract for commercial products. Later, parts of the standard have been adopted to XML Linking Language and to some commercial advanced browsers for creating customized applications.

1998 In February, the eXtensible Markup Language (XML) got the recommendation status in the W3C. XML is a subset of SGML and especially designed for Web (W3C, 2004a)

2001 In June, XML Linking Language (XLink) specification got the recommendation status in the W3C. XLink defines extended links with multiple linking and linkbase facilities and as such brings the possibility to implement more versatile link structures, already defined in earlier days' hypermedia systems such as Intermedia, on the Web. XLink is increasingly moving the Web towards an open hypermedia approach. However, XLink is quite sophisticated and is applied mainly in customized applications. DocZilla by Citec Information Inc. is an example of commercial browser/editor supporting multi-ended links and linkbases (W3C, 2004d; DocZilla, 2004).

2001- Peter Brusilovsky presented a two-level categorization for adaptive systems: adaptation to user's behaviour and adaptation to the client device. Brusilovsky and his research group at Carnegie Mellon University and nowadays at University of Pittsburgh are developing methods for adaptive Web. (Brusilovsky et al., 2002)

5th Generation: Mobile Web and Semantic Web are developing

2001 Tim Berners-Lee defined the next generation of the Web, which he calls the Semantic Web. W3C's Semantic Web -activity aims to develop Web technologies to have data

	defined and linked in a way that allows it to be used by machines, not just for display purposes, but for integration and reuse of information across various applications. (Berners-Lee et al., 2001)
2001	The Oxford Internet Institute (OII) was founded (OII, 2004). OII aims to become the world's leading multi-disciplinary academic centre focused on furthering understanding of the economic, political, institutional, scientific, legal and other social factors shaping the Internet and its implications for society.
2002-	Mobile Internet starts to provide new means for working and learning. Harri Ketamo at Tampere University of Technology, Pori, has developed and evaluated xTask environment for user and platform adaptation in Web-based learning environments. (Ketamo, 2002)
2002-	XLink becomes a bridge between open hypermedia research and W3C communities. Both communities have a great potential to learn from each other. On the one hand, hypermedia research community begins to use the Web and XLink as a test bed for developing and evaluating more complex link structures. On the other hand, W3C community could utilize even more efficiently the hypermedia research work already done. XLink extensions such as support for multimedia synchronization, mapping between open hypermedia interchange format and an XLink linkbase, and time-sensitive linking mechanisms are published. (Heimbürger, 2004; Grønbæk et al., 2000; Muchaluat-Saade et al., 2002)
2004	In February, the Semantic Web technologies got the recommendation status in the W3C (W3C, 2004b).
2004	The mobile computing has two different starting points. The first is the computer manufacturers. One of the first developers for mobile devices has been Psion (Organiser since 1984) and Apple Computer (Newton, 1993). These devices did not have any communications capabilities. They were more like electronic calendars although it was possible to draw and write with the Newton. The second starting point is mobile communication device manufacturers. In 1996 Nokia introduced the world's first all-in-one communicator, the Nokia 9000. It had many features seen in PDAs in addition to the GSM communications capabilities. Today also the PDAs have an integrated communication

	technologies (such as GSM, GPRS or WLAN). This year (2004) Nokia have introduced its newest Communicator with both WLAN and GSM/GPRS interfaces.
Future	Openness of computer and information systems, automatic integration and reuse of information across various applications and devices, possibilities for cultural localization, context awareness with content personalization and adaptation, multimodal interfaces and facilities for authoring and managing versatile link structures are some of the most important challenges for the network of the future.

From the chronology we can see that information and communication technologies have been used in learning applications in many ways. Almost every new technology is to be applied in learning context. For example, HyperCard became very popular among schools soon after it was published. The students could easily do their presentations and group work using Macintosh and HyperCard. The popularity of HyperCard was based mainly on two things: first, it was free software included for every Macintosh and second, it was very easy to program. These two principles characterize also the World Wide Web. Today, many features included in commercial learning environments and learning platforms have already been present for example in Augment, PLATO, Intermedia and Guide. From this point of view the mobility and Semantic Web are new paradigms - a great deal of research and experiments are needed in order to launch the full potential of these technologies in learning.

Next we will focus on how our understanding of learning has changed over time.

3. DEVELOPMENT OF LEARNING THEORIES

In the previous section we presented a timeline of several technologies that have influenced CAL. How the human mind learns is still an open research issue that has been studied from many perspectives. In this chapter we present a simplified timeline that describes the development of learning theories during the last century.

The learning theories can be described with a line segment with two ends. On one end there is behaviourist learning model and on the other end there is cognitive learning model (i.e. constructivist learning model). In between, there are numerous learning models mixing features of behaviourism and constructivism. The line represents also a simplified timeline in such that behaviourist learning models were commonly accepted in the beginning of 1900 and the constructive learning models are much newer ideas. One of the developers of behaviourism was B. F. Skinner (Graham, 2002). In general, behaviourism says that our learning is based on stimulus response method which means that by certain stimulus there should be a certain response. One example of behaviourist learning is learning by memorizing things by heart. In computer software behaviourist programs were often of drill type: the student had to answer to a series of questions computer asked often in quick pace.

In contrast, cognitive learning model concerns more on the learning process itself. One of the first cognitive scientists has been Noam Chomsky (Thagard, 2002). It is widely accepted that networked learning should be based on cognitive learning model. An example of this in CAL could be simulation software where the student learns by studying the simulator and by experimenting with the controls of the simulation.

In the end of 1980s a new design method for CAL were launched. Crossley's and Green's (1985, 1987) method for designing lessonware were applied to many CAL developed at that time. It introduced an "open market place" where the learner could "walk" and go to small "shops" to learn. The learner could control the learning pace and route. There were also other design methods for lessonware that were based on cognitive learning model. It can be said that the use of these design methods had positive impact on the quality of learning software.

All these methods were forgotten (at least for a while) when World Wide Web appeared. Suddenly teachers started to design HTML-pages for learning purposes. The structure of the HTML-pages was not designed from pedagogical point of view. Instead, the new technology was used to publish lecture notes on the Web.

Nowadays quite a great deal of research is looking at collaborative learning. Learning is not seen only as an individual process. Learning is based on collaboration and communication. One example of this is networked learning environments that support bulletin boards and online conferencing.

When designing and studying new technologies, for example linking methods, we should keep the lessons learned in mind and try to focus on pedagogically new and meaningful ideas of applying new technologies. We should also remember the associative nature of human thinking.

4. HYPERTEXT LINKING: MEANS FOR IMPLEMENTING ASSOCIATIVE INFORMATION STRUCTURES

4.1 Extended links

Hypertext is a tool for building and using associative information structures. Pieces of knowledge can be assembled in different ways according to different perspectives of users. Hypertext links are implementations of relationships within and among sets of data. In fact, links are themselves important pieces of data that need to be authored, stored, maintained, delivered and used just like other data. Many earlier hypertext systems had a versatile linking structure. For example, the Intermedia system had structured links with attributes such as types and keywords (Yankelovich et al., 1985). Links in Intermedia were bi-directional and it was possible to get an overview of the link structure in a hypertext document. Intermedia also included the concept of a linkbase. These features are still not widely found on the Web. The linking mechanism on the Web is still weak, although there are strengths in the HTML linking. HTML has an easy syntax and it is simple to implement. However, the design of Web pages has concentrated rather on getting the right look than to constructing useful structures.

Hypertext link management has been a matter of serious concern in the open hypermedia (OH) research community for over ten years now. When links are embedded in documents, as they are now in the Web, there are several disadvantages which affect the management effort of contents and their relations. Open hypermedia research and the recent XML Linking Language (XLink) recommendation in the W3C indicate that the solution is to separate the links from the content by means of an external hypermedia linkbase architecture. In addition to linkbases, XLink defines semantic, behaviour and traversal link attributes, and multi-ended links (Figure 1).

XLink's extended link can include attributes reflecting the relationships between the starting and ending resources of a link. Examples are user id, place, time and information type. Multi-ended links can also contain multi-ended links, which makes multiple link networks possible. Some of these features already existed in early days' stand-alone hypertext systems. XLink attempts to adjust these linking facilities to the Web.

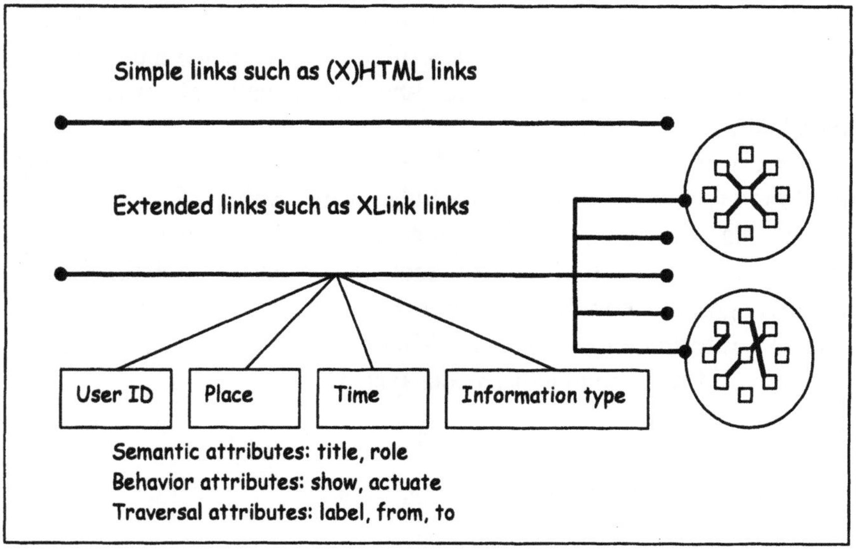

Figure 1. A HTML link versus an XLink link.

4.2 Examples of applying extended link structures to the design of training materials

If the links are kept separate from the contents, more flexibility and control is achieved, such as (a) contents and fragments of contents can be linked automatically without changing them in any way, (b) alternative sets of links can be associated with the same content according to the needs of different contexts, (c) collections of links can be filtered on demand and (d) link integrity can be verified automatically.

The linkbase architecture allows collaborative annotation, for example the common set of learning materials on the Web (W3C, 2004c). Linkbase architecture also enables the creation of more complex link structures such as combinations of multi-ended links and linkbases, and thus is necessary from a link management point of view. Versatile link structures can be applied to contextual composing, delivering and using assemblies of training materials on the Web. Examples of possible applications are: (a) composing step-by-step instructions in industrial training situations onsite, for example in simulated trouble-shooting situations, (b) providing different views to training materials for example chronological, cultural and environmental views, (c) a possibility to switch between a novice-, an intermediate- or an expert-view depending on the user's level of know-how, (d) time-based teaching of history, historical events and relations between them, (e) semantic relations to topics, for instance the topic "the Finnish composer

Jean Sibelius" in music teaching can be an anchor to a four-ended link: events, persons, places, sample library of compositions, (e) multilingual and multicultural aspects of applications, and (f) curricula of universities and students' study programs.

Hypertext linking has developed from simple to versatile linking in stand-alone systems, back to simple links in the Web, and now proceeding again towards more complex link structures. First implementations are to be in extranet and intranet environments that are subsets of the Web. XLink and alike languages are enriching linking methods and tools for constructing associative information structures. They are also developing the Web towards a world wide open hypermedia system.

5. CONCLUSIONS

The human mind seems to be associative by its nature. This has been observed in many contexts and has been formulated in network models of human memory (Parsaye et al., 1989). The natural tendency of human mind to build complex associative structures differs from the linear way in which information is generally organized and presented, for example in books. Hypertext offers us a tool for building and using associative information structures.

It must be remembered that learning happens inside our brain – this process can be aided using technologies. However, the nature of learning is in thinking and doing. Thinking is an associative process and it can be expressed in computer by using hypermedia links that encompass the rich semantics of relationships of different things. When designing and studying new technologies, in this case especially linking methods, we should keep the lessons learned in mind and try to focus on pedagogically new and meaningful ideas of applying new technologies.

REFERENCES

Berk, E. and Devlin, J. (eds.), 1991. *Hypertext/hypermedia handbook.* New York: Intertext Publications. 583 p.

Berners-Lee, T., 1999. *Weaving the Web. The original design and ultimate destiny of the World Wide Web.* New York, Harper San Francisco. 226 p.

Berners-Lee, T., Hendler, J. and Lassila, O., 2001. The Semantic Web. *Scientific American,* Vol. 284, No. 5, pp. 28 – 37.

Brusilovsky, P., Stock, O. and Strapparava, C. (eds.), 2002. *Adaptive hypermedia and adaptive Web-based systems.* Lecture Notes in Computer Science 1892, Berlin, Springer-Verlag. 422 p.

Burch, R. O., 2001. Effective web design and core communication issues: The missing components in Web-based distance education. *Journal of Educational Multimedia and Hypermedia*, Vol. 10, No. 4, pp. 357 – 367.

Bush, V., 1945. As we may think. *Atlantic Monthly*, Vol. 176, No. 1, pp. 101 – 108.

Carlson, R. D. and Repman, J., 2002. Activating Web-based e-learning. *International Journal on E-learning*, Vol. 1, No. 2, pp. 7 – 10.

Carr, L. et al., 1995. The distributed link service: A tool for publishers, authors and readers. In: *The 4th International World Wide Web Conference: The Web Revolution*, Boston, MA, O'Reilly. Pp. 647 – 656.

Crestani, F. and Ntioudis, S. P., 2002. User centered evaluation of an automatically constructed Hyper-TextBook. *Journal of Educational Multimedia and Hypermedia*, Vol. 11, No. 1, pp. 3 – 19.

Crossley, K. and Green, L., 1985. *A Practical Guide For Teachers: Designing Computer Lessonware*, Canada.

Crossley K. and Green L., 1987. *Lessonware. Käytännön opas opetusohjelmien laatimiseen.* WSOY. Juva. (In Finnish)

DocZilla, 2004. DocZilla, [referenced 1.3.2004], <URL: http://www.doczilla.com/>.

Engelbart, D. C., 1963. A conceptual framework for the augmentation of man's intellect.In: Howerton, P. W. and Weeks, D. C. (eds.). *Vistas in information handling*. Volume 1. The augmentation of man's intellect by machine. Washington, D.C., Spartan Books. Pp. 1 – 29.

Graham, G., 2002. Behaviorism, *The Stanford Encyclopedia of Philosophy* (Fall 2002 Edition), Edward N. Zalta (ed.), [referenced 1.3.2004], <URL: http://plato.stanford.edu/archives/fall2002/entries/behaviorism/ >

Grønbæk, K. and Trigg, R. H., 1999. *From Web to workplace: Designing open hypermedia systems*. Boston, MA, The MIT Press Books. 424 pp.

Grønbæk, K., Sloth, L. and Bouvin, N. O., 2000. Open hypermedia as user controlled meta data for the web. In *Proceedings of the 9th International World Wide Web Conference*, May 2000, Amsterdam, Holland. Pp. 553 – 566.

Halasz, F., 1988. Reflections on Note Cards: seven issues for the next generation of hypermedia systems. *Communications of the ACM*, Vol. 31, No. 7, pp. 836 – 852.

Harley, K., 2001. Learning strategies and hypermedia instruction. *Journal of Educational Multimedia and Hypermedia*, Vol. 10, No. 3, pp. 285 – 305.

Hede, A., 2002. An integrated model of multimedia effects on learning. *Journal of Educational Multimedia and Hypermedia*, Vol. 11, No. 2, pp. 177 – 191.

Heimbürger, A., 2004. Time-sensitive relationship management in technical manuals. Case: Maintenance schedules. Submitted to: *The 14th European-Japanese Conference on Information Modelling and Knowledge Bases* (EJC 2004), May 31 – June 4, 2003, Skoevde University, Sweden. 20 p.

Hobbs, D. L., 2002. A constructivist approach to Web course design: A review of the literature. *International Journal on E-Learning*, Vol. 1, No. 2, pp. 60 – 65.

ISO 8879., 1986. *Information processing – Text and office systems – Standard generalized markup language (SGML)*. Geneva: International Organization for Standardization. 155 p.

ISO/IEC 10744., 1997. *Information processing – Hypermedia/Time-based Structuring Language (HyTime)* - 2d edition [referred 1.3.2004] <URL: http://www.ornl.gov/sgml/wg8/docs/n1920//>.

Ketamo, H., 2002. *User and platform adaptation in web-based learning environments.* Tampere University of Technology Publications 381, Tampere, Tampere University of Technology. 142 p.

Muchaluat-Saade, D. C., Rodrigues, R. F. and Soares, L. F. G., 2002. XConnector: Extending XLink to provide multimedia synchronization. *Document Engineering (DocEng '02)*, November 8 – 9, 2002; McLean, Virginia; USA. Pp. 49 – 56.

Mullier, D., Hobbs, D. and Moore, D., 2002. Identifying and using hypermedia browsing patterns. *Journal of Educational Multimedia and Hypermedia*, Vol. 11, No. 1, pp. 31 – 50.

Multisilta, J., 1996. *Hypermedia learning environment for mathematics*. Tampere University of Technology Publications 183, Tampere, Tampere University of Technology. 221 p.

Nelson, T. H., 1987. *Literary Machines*. Edition 87.1, San Antonio, TX, Project Xanadu. 263 p.

Nelson, T. H., 2004. Home Page of Ted Nelson, [referenced 1.3.2004], <URL: http://www.xanadu.com.au/ted/>

Nielsen, J., 1993. *Usability engineering*. San Francisco, CA, Morgan Kaufmann Publishers, Inc. 362 p.

Nielsen, J., 2000. *Designing Web usability*. Indianapolis, IN, New Readers Publishing. 419 p.

Nievergelt, J., 1980. A pragmatic introduction to courseware design. *IEEE Computer*, Vol. 13, No. 9, pp. 7-21.

Ohl, T. M., 2001. An interaction-centric learning model. *Journal of Educational Multimedia and Hypermedia*, Vol. 10, No. 4, pp. 311 – 332.

OII, 2004. Oxford Internet Institute, [referenced 1.3.2004], <URL: http://www.oii.ox.ac.uk/about/>

Oliver, R. and McLoughlin, C., 2001. Exploring the practise and development of generic skills through Web-based learning. *Journal of Educational Multimedia and Hypermedia*, Vol. 10, No. 3, pp. 207 – 225.

Pantages, A., 1976. Control Data's education offering: "Plato would have enjoyed PLATO". *Datamation*, Vol. 22, No. 5, pp. 183 – 187.

Parsaye, K. et al., 1989. *Intelligent databases*. New York, NY, John Wiley & Sons, Inc. 479 p.

Thagard, P., 2002. Cognitive Science, *The Stanford Encyclopedia of Philosophy* (Winter 2002 Edition), Edward N. Zalta (ed.), [referenced 1.3.2004], <URL: http://plato.stanford.edu/archives/win2002/entries/cognitive-science/ >

Van Dam, A., 1988 Hypertext '87 Keynote Address, Special issue: Hypertext. *Communications of the ACM*, Vol. 31, No. 7, pp. 887 – 895.

W3C, 2004a. Extensible Markup Language (XML), [referenced 1.3.2004], <URL: http://www.w3.org/XML/>

W3C, 2004b. Semantic Web, [referenced 1.3.2004], <URL: http://www.w3.org/2001/sw/>

W3C, 2004c. The Annotea Project, [referenced 1.3.2004], <URL: http://www.w3.org/2001/Annotea/>

W3C, 2004d. XML Linking Language (XLink), [referenced 1.3.2004], <URL: http://www.w3.org/TR/xlink/>

Yankelovich, N. et al., 1985. Reading and writing the electronic book. *IEEE Computer*, Vol. 18, No. 10, pp. 15 – 30.

KEYBOARD TRAINING IN AN INFORMATION ORIENTED SOCIETY

Hajime Ohiwa
Keio University, Japan
E-mail: ohiwa@sfc.keio.ac.jp

Abstract: Importance of the mother language support of the computer is pointed out and input method for the Japanese language is described both from historical and practical viewpoint. It is argued that early training of keyboard is essential but it should be done after hand-writing is well established by schoolchildren.

Key words: Touch-typing; Mother Language Support; Large Character Set

1. MOTHER LANGUAGE SHOULD BE SUPPORTED ON A COMPUTER

Although the cost of a computer decreased, it cannot be widely used by common people unless the character set of their mother language is fully supported. It can easily be achieved for most European languages in which only twenty-six-letter alphabets are used.

In Asia, the situation is different. For example, the Japanese language uses not only two types of phonograms (Kana) called Hiragana and Katakana but also uses several thousands of Chinese characters called Kanji. This large character set could not be fully supported by early computers and only Katakana was implemented.

The traditional Japanese typists employ a hunt and peck method of keyboarding because of the large character set. Due to this cumbersome operation and the slow speed, the use of a typewriter has not been as common in Japan as in the Western society where the typing operation is achieved with visual contact with the keyboard.

Word processing is the central part of the use of computer by a common people (Ohiwa, 1987), and it should be the center of computer literacy education. In 1978, the first Japanese word processor was introduced, and full support of Japanese language was realized. Until the 1990s, this special purpose computer was widely used in Japan, but now its function can be realized by software on a personal computer.

2. INPUT METHODS FOR THE JAPANESE LANGUAGE

2.1 Various input methods were proposed but the keyboard was chosen

Although the Japanese character set was supported by a computer, how to input the character set was the problem. In early Japanese word processors, in addition to common keyboards for the Kana and Kanji alphabets, a special hardware was used as a natural extension of traditional Japanese typewriter. However, the keyboard gradually had gained popularity and ultimately the special input hardware disappeared because of the additional cost and inefficiency of input operations. However, the main reason for keyboard usage is that the way to use keyboard for inputting the character set has become sophisticated as described below and now Japanese users feel comfortable with it.

2.2 Kana-Kanji conversion or consultation to a dictionary has become standard in Japan

The popular method for inputting Japanese language is Kana to Kanji conversion method in which, for inputting Kanji, its pronunciation is inputted by a Kana or an alphabet keyboard and then corresponding Kanjis are shown on a screen by consulting a dictionary. The target Kanji is then pointed out by the user. This interactivity comes from the homonymy of Kanjis. The following is an example to show the problem.

貴社の記者が汽車で帰社した

Kisha no kisha ga kisha de Kisha shita.

(The reporter of your company returned to his office by train.)

In this example, "kisha" may be the reporter, your company, train, or returned to his office. Various technical efforts were made to attack this problem and the method has been very detailed.

2.3 Two-stroke methods

Kanji can be input by using the two-stroke method. A Kana keyboard has forty-eight keys and if a Kanji is assigned by two keys, two thousand three hundred and four (= 48 x 48) Kanjis may be uniquely determined by typing two keys. Many such methods were proposed and used by professional people to input a large number of Kanjis (Yamada, 1983, Ohiwa and Tatsuoka, 1990). Among them T-code by H. Yamada (Yamada, 1983) has been used by computer scientists and TUT-code by H. Ohiwa (Ohiwa and Tatsuoka, 1990) has been used among the printing industry operators.

The advantage of these two-stroke methods is that no interactive activity with computer is needed and that their input efficiency is as good as that of alphabetical typing.

It may seem difficult to memorize key sequences for inputting Kanjis, but it is not as serious as it looks. The number of Kanjis a person uses is relatively small and in fact, it is about four hundred. Therefore, input sequences may be learned within a hundred hours of training. This four hundred Kanji set is different for each person and in total two thousand Kanji sets are used by Japanese people.

3. TOUCH-TYPING IS EASY TO LEARN BUT WRONG METHODS PROLIFERATE

3.1 Touch-typing of keyboard can be done after an hour of training

For getting the ability for touch-typing alphabets, only an hour of practice is enough (Ohiwa and Tatsuoka 1990). The point of practice is as follows:

1. Never look at the keyboard.
2. Use the same fingering,
3. Always return to the home position,
4. Be conscious of the alphabet to be typed.

If these points are kept in mind of the trainee and designed sequence of keying is done for an hour, the ability for touch-typing alphabets can be established. One of such training sequence is as follows:

JKJ JLJ J;J JHJ; JUJ JIJ JOJ JPJ JYJ: JMJ J,J J.J J/J JNJ:
KJK KLK K;K KHK: KUK KIK KOK KPK KYK: KMK K,K K.K K/K KNK:
LJL LKL L;L LHL: LUL LIL LOL LPL LYL: LML L,L L.L L/L LNL.

The first line is the practice for the letter "J" and the second for "K" and the third for "L". During the practice of "J", other letters typed by the right hand is pre-trained and during the practice of "K" and the following letters, the letter "J" is refreshed. After practicing every letters in an hour or two depending on the motor-skill, the ability of touch-typing is established.

This practice is not for memorizing the keyboard layout. After a practice, the fingers memorize how to type. In other words, if asked to type a letter, he/she can type correctly. It is a motor action memorization and not a mental act.

Because it is so easy to learn, it is very easy to lose. Typing everyday for a week or two must be followed for making the learning permanent. This can easily be done nowadays because e-mail and other typing activities have become so necessary.

There are several software packages for typing training, but many of them were developed by a hunt and peck typist. Therefore, their understanding of typing is not that of touch-typing and the target of the practice is to memorize the keyboard layout. It is not helpful for acquiring a touch-typing skill. In fact, if a typist is asked to tell the name of the character of the alphabet associated with some key, he/she cannot answer.

3.2 Typing skill requires several hundreds of hours practice

Although acquiring the ability for touch-typing is very easy, it takes several hundreds of hours for acquiring the skill in which typing become an automatic action and the spelling of a word, for example, does not come out to the typist's mind during the typing operation. Once such skill is acquired, typing becomes very comfortable activity and a voice recognition system, for example, which is eagerly desired by those who cannot do touch-typing, is not desirable, because roughly speaking, vocal action is twice as laborious as typing action.

3.3 Kanji input without consultation to a dictionary should be used mainly

The two-stroke method should be used for touch-typing Japanese from the viewpoint of efficiency of inputting the mother language. However, to get the skill it is not as easy as alphabetical typing, because two strokes are required for inputting the Japanese characters. If touch-typing is confined to Kana characters, the ability for touch-typing can be acquired after an hour of practice, because the number of combinations of characters is limited to less than hundred. Those who do not input Japanese frequently may use the Kana-Kanji conversion after acquiring the touch-typing skill for Kana.

Those who write Japanese on a computer with Kana-Kanji conversion have many troubles during the conversion process. If he/she concentrates on the contents to be typed, he/she often overlooks the wrong selection of Kanji. This often happens when there are similar meaning Kanjis with same pronunciation. If he/she concentrates on the selection, his/her concentration on the contents is disturbed. Therefore, those heavy users should acquire the touch-typing skill of two-stroke method.

Considering the number of Kanjis one person uses, the touch-typing ability may be acquired less than a hundred hours of training. Although this may seem long for practicing, it is reasonable if you consider the time required for acquiring the skill for Western languages is several hundred of hours.

4. TOUCH-TYPING FOR EVERYONE

Although touch-typing is very easy to practice most people, including Westerners, do not employ touch-typing. This is because its ease is not understood even by IT education professionals. Once its ease is well known, it would be done by every personal computer user.

If someone who does hunt and peck typing knows the ease of touch-typing and undertakes its training, he/she can acquire the ability but it is very hard for him/her to continue touch-typing. The new way of typing requires severe concentration but the hunt and peck method is still comfortable for him/her. If touch-typing is not continued, the acquired ability disappears immediately.

This fact shows the keyboard training should be done at the very beginning of using a keyboard, because once hunt and peck method is established, it is very hard to replace. This means that every IT teacher should be able to teach touch-typing.

Another issue for keyboard training is when it should be done. If it is done at the lower elementary school level, schoolchildren would not do hand-writing, because hand-writing requires harder skills than keyboarding. If letters must be input to the computer by those children whose hand writing skill is poor, it should be done through mouse or pen operations through a letter matrix on the screen.

When keyboard training should be done? The answer would be after establishing a hand-writing skill. Another important point is that teachers should use touch-typing even if he/she does not teach typing. If he/she types by hunt and peck method, children thinks what the teacher does is right, which is a serious mistake from which it is very hard to recover.

REFERENCES

Ohiwa, H., 1987, "Keyboard Training as a Basis for Computer Literacy Education", in: *Microcomputers in Secondary Education*, S. Moriguti, S. Ohtsuki, and T Furugori, ed., North-Holland, Amsterdam, pp.339-342.

Ohiwa, H. and H. Tatsuoka, 1990, "Keyboards for Inputting Japanese Text and Training Methods for Touch-typing", *J. Information Processing*, Vol. 13, No. 1, pp. 35-43.

Yamada, H., 1987, "Certain Problems Associated with the Design of Input Keyboards for Japanese Writing", Chapter 13, *Cognitive Aspects of Skilled Typewriting*, W. E. Cooper, ed., Springer-Verlag, New York, pp.305-407.

STUDYING EDUCATIONAL COMPUTING PROJECTS

Challenges and Opportunities

Mary E. Hopper
Lesley University, USA
E-mail: mhopper@mail.lesley.edu

Abstract: This paper describes how a long-term project has evolved from a qualitative research study carried out in the early 1990s to the point of transition where it is today. The long-term goal of the project has been to improve the viability of educational computing projects by identifying and disseminating effective and sustainable strategies. The initial study took place between the years 1990-1993. Information from interviews with 19 key participants and supplemental documents were used to explore the educational, technical and organizational contexts of a number of projects. In each project, attempts to reach unique discipline and learner oriented goals afforded by new computing capabilities led to unforeseen technical challenges that became intertwined with issues related to traditional organizational structures. Limitations encountered in the original study's methodology drove this project to transform into an initiative to use negotiation and cooperation to collect and compare historical data about educational computing projects.

Key words: Distributed computing; Academic computing; Historical case studies.

1. INTRODUCTION

The goal of improving the viability of educational computing projects by identifying and disseminating effective strategies has historically been a common enterprise (McClintock, 1986; Taylor, 1980). However, when personal desktop computers became common in the early 1980s, pressures from business and government resulted in more intense efforts to determine what had gone wrong in the past and what could be done to insure future efforts would be successful. The report *POWER ON: New Tools for*

Teaching and Learning (OTA, 1988) described how the number of computers in education had been steadily increasing, but that their numbers and quality were still too low for them to have a large impact across the curriculum at that time. The authors of that report relied upon beliefs about the problems in past initiatives to support the following recommendations for future efforts:

- Expanding the amount and capability of technology in schools to increase student access;
- Providing training and support for teachers;
- Encouraging innovation and improvement in educational software; and
- Supporting research, development, demonstration, and evaluation, with emphasis on ties between research and the classroom. (OTA, 1988, p. 4)

These broad suggestions were based upon an extensive analysis of reports from older projects and highlighted problems that thwarted previous efforts. Addressing the issues would certainly be prerequisites for insuring the success of new educational computing initiatives. However, it was increasingly clear that new educational computing initiatives would be using networked computing environments and software capable of accessing and manipulating many widely distributed databases of linked text, graphics, sound and video (Molnar, 1990). This would represent a revolution in the computing paradigm like that which occurred in the shift from mainframe computers to microcomputers in the 1970s and 1980s. Would it be enough for new educational computing projects to address the flaws in earlier projects, or would they fail due to unforeseen problems that were a function of the new computing paradigm?

Personal experience with creating the educational computing project ESCAPE, an information system for engineers implemented within a distributed computing environment at Purdue University in 1989-1990 convinced this researcher that there would be new problems that would threaten the success of educational computing projects in distributed computing environments (Hopper, LeBold, & Feghali, 1991). This was the motivating force behind the decision to undertake a study to explore how problems that characterized previous educational computing initiatives became intertwined with unique new problems that were a function of distributed computing (Hopper, 1993).

2. METHODS

It was critical to gather information from the few existing pockets of expertise in using distributed computing environments for educational projects. Academic computing organizations at Purdue University, Brown University (Meyrowitz, 1986; Yankelovich, Meyrowitz & VanDam, 1985) and the Massachusetts Institute of Technology (Arfman & Roden, 1992; Champine, 1991; Lerman, 1987) had invested in creating distributed networked computing systems beginning in the late 1970s. The educational projects created using those environments were ending and ready to be analyzed with hindsight by their participants by 1990. This study focused on courseware projects rather than systems software, programming languages or authoring tools.

The following research questions guided this study:

- What were the relationships between the educational, technical, and organizational contexts of courseware?
- What were the educational goals of the courseware?
- Did the goals focus more upon discipline-oriented outcomes, or upon broader outcomes for the learners?
- What educational considerations influenced technical decisions about courseware?
- What were pragmatic technical issues that emerged during courseware projects?
- What were key technical characteristics that determined the viability of courseware?
- What were the relationships between the roles, tasks, and the timing of tasks?

The following projects, organizations and participants were the focus of this study:

Project: ESCAPE (HyperCard, HyperNews, Gohper, WWW)
Organizations: Educational Research and Information Systems, Freshman Engineering, Purdue University
Participants: Thomas Putnam, William LeBold, Robert Lawler, Mary Hopper, Sherman Ward, Judy Rehwinkel, Robert Tillotson
(LeBold, Hopper & Feghali, 1991)

Project: Context32 (Intermedia, StorySpace, WWW)
Organizations: Institute for Research and Information Scholarship, Brown University
Participants: Nicole Yankelovich, Paul Kahn, George Landow
(Beeman, et.al., 1987; Landow, 1989)

Project: TODOR (Athena, BLOX) & Mechanics 2.01 (Athena, cT)
Organizations: Athena and Academic Computing and Aero/Astro Engineering, Massachusetts Institute of Technology
Participants: Gregory Jackson, Naomi Schmidt, Janet Daly, Anne Lavin, Laurence Bucciarelli
(Murman, LaVin & Ellis, 1988; McCune, 1989; Murman, 1987; Trilling, 1988) (Bucciarelli, 1992; Bucciarelli & LaVin, 1992)

Project: Physical Geology Tutor (Athena, AthenaMuse)
Organizations: Center for Educational Computing Initiatives and Civil Engineering, Massachusetts Institute of Technology
Participants: Steven Lerman, Benjamin Davis, Evelyn Schlusselberg, Pat Kinnicutt
(Einstein, 1991; Kinnicutt, 1992)

The main data collection strategy used in the study was in-depth interviews with key developers and managers of the organizations that supported the projects (Marshall & Rossman, 1989, p. 94). The researcher's personal conversations with participants illuminated events and relationships that were critical during courseware development, but were not frequently or freely written about in published accounts. Every interview was audio or video taped. Once the tape was transcribed, interview logs were divided into segments based on topics of conversations.

A continuous process of literature review was essential to continue apace of numerous references provided by participants. The accumulated documents were used extensively to conduct "historical analysis" (Borg and Gall et al, 1989, p. 403). This allowed triangulation between more accounts than were available through interviews alone.

The passages from interviews were combined with selected passages from the project director's and producer's other published reports and publications to result in the total passages that were included in the original research report. The total amount of taped data collected during interviews, and the relative proportion of transcribed passages from those tapes that were actually included in the original research report are represented in Table 1 below. The complete data collection process resulted in a series of historical case studies that captured participant's expert recollections, insights and hind sights about the development of the educational projects in early distributed computing environments.

Table 1. Data Collected, Transcribed and Included in the Study

Projects	Hours of Taped Interviews	Passages Transcribed	Passages in Report from Interviews	Passages in Report from Publications	Total Passages in Report
ESCAPE	9.5 (Video)	50	22	60	82
Context32	3.5 (Audio)	23	9	45	54
TODOR/201	6.0 (Audio)	30	22	35	57
Geo. Tutor	4.75 (Audio)	26	19	20	39
Total Data	23.75	129	72	169	232

3. RESULTS

Triangulation among data obtained through interviews and analysis of documents allowed this researcher to determine that each of the projects were characterized by simultaneous attention to a consistent set of key factors across their educational, technical and organizational contexts. The major factor in the success of courseware initiatives was the degree to which they found ways to address their educational and technical requirements within the constraints of the organizational considerations.

3.1 Educational Context

The participants in this study were first and foremost concerned with the educational nature of their endeavor. All of the projects studied began with goals for providing both improved representations of the discipline and increased learner involvement. Successful projects tried to provide a significantly different experience than could be provided through more traditional means. Participants in this study of successful courseware endeavors developed explicit rationales describing how the computer based tools met their educational goals in ways that could not be done in any other way as effectively, efficiently or cheaply. An orientation towards thoughtful implementation of technology based on its ability to serve broader, preexisting educational goals was a predominant theme throughout the projects studied. This careful attention to the "educational" nature of computing projects exerted a powerful influence upon technical and organizational decisions.

3.2 Technical Context

Critical technical characteristics of software included appropriate functionality, usability for interaction and creation, and adaptability for the change inherent in distributed computing environments.

Balancing these issues with the educational goals at hand took a great deal of effort and forethought by those closely associated with projects. To forget about technical requirements was to ensure the limited success of a project. However, another danger was to become so concerned about solving technical problems that sight was lost of the educational goals.

The selection of software was primarily based upon its ability to represent a particular aspect of the discipline at hand. Then regardless of the types of software that projects used, how well the software supported the creation of courseware and the interaction of users became a major consideration. According to the degree of emphasis on learner oriented goals, the degree of usability for the author or the learner were also important attributes that were considered as selection criteria before the package was adopted. In cases where ease of use was not considered ahead of time, it became a major problem once the courseware was under construction (Hopper, 1994).

The adaptability of courseware so as to preserve availability by accommodating change was a significant issue. For example, the Context32 project was deeply affected by the lack of adaptability of the Intermedia software. Despite the immense amount of work and educational thought that went into creating Intermedia, it's lack of adaptability ultimately caused it's demise. In the following passage, Paul Kahn, then director of the Institute for Information and Scholarship, portrayed the adaptability issues that brought the conclusion of the Intermedia project:

> "The news has been both good and bad. The good news has been that this ambitious design has been accomplished without special hardware or operating system software. Pre-3.0 Intermedia had required a version of the UNIX operating system for the IBM RT PC that was not generally available. It had also been built on a layer of software and a database management system that presented formidable licensing constraints for distribution outside of Brown University. All of these constraints had been overcome in Intermedia 3.0, and as a result over 200 licensed copies were distributed in 1989 and 1990. However, the bad news has been that, despite it general availability since 1988, Apple's UNIX has never been the operating system of choice for most Macintosh users. The cost of a Macintosh operating system is included in the price of the computer. A/UX must be purchased separately and has always required significantly more RAM (at a time when memory was very expensive) and more hard disk than the Macintosh operating system. Running A/UX added between $2,000 and 4,000 to the cost a Macintosh II workstation. In addition, the kind of a high-speed transparent network file access that makes the collaborative features of Intermedia possible require Ethernet

hardware. Up through the summer of 1990 Intermedia had been one of the few applications that ran under A/UX and one of only a handful that made use of the Macintosh Toolbox to present a graphical user interface. In the summer of 1990, Apple Computer made changes to A/UX version 2.0 that made it incompatible with Intermedia. By that time, support for further development of Intermedia had ended. To run Intermedia, users have had to maintain or locate a version of A/UX that is no longer supported by Apple." (Launhardt & Kahn, 1991, pp. 13-14)

The Intermedia project officially ended in 1991 while this study was taking place, and George Landow was porting Context32 to Eastgate System's Story Space hypertext software. This resulted in the loss of the functionality of collaboration over a network, but it also resulted in the project becoming widely available. Ultimately, availability was the goal.

Projects that used the Athena computing environment at MIT also experienced problems with adaptability. The biggest problems were due to incompatibilities in X-Windows System 10 and System 11 (Stewart, 1989). In fact, the TODOR project included in this study was one of the few that survived the changes, and that survival was attributed to the presence of a member of the Athena development team on that project.

3.3 Organizational Context

The factors in the organizational contexts were far more critical than had been anticipated prior to the initiation of this research. The reasons for this were most salient for projects at MIT. The educational projects that used Athena needed to cope with continuous change and expansion of the underlying system, and thus also needed to change in order to survive. The discontinuation of either delivery or modification marked the end of a project because courseware quickly fell from disuse to unusable. To insure that the project was used, updated and expanded, authors needed to continually find ways to acquire critical resources. The dilemma was to find ways both inside and outside of traditional organizational structures to overcome the inherent lack of existing support for courseware development in academic settings. Successful projects recast learners as authors, while authors were recast as managers of educational, technical and organizational factors that needed to be continuously balanced (Hopper, 1997).

In summary, each project's attempts to reach unique discipline and learner oriented goals afforded by new computing capabilities led to unforeseen technical challenges that became intertwined with issues related to traditional organizational structures for distributing and managing human, technological, and financial resources in academic organizations. When educational decisions presented technical challenges, successful projects developed organizational structures to address the challenges.

4. DISCUSSION

The results of this study yielded valuable advice about how to implement educational projects in distributed computing environments and was applicable to the World Wide Web as it emerged. However, there was also another important outcome of this study. Later reflections by the author and feedback from the participants made it apparent that it would be valuable to systematically gather and integrate increasingly elaborate, detailed and older data about educational computing projects. The goal of this would be to document and understand the complex historical contexts that led to the success of ongoing projects across multiple generations of technology.

Projects increasingly have a cyclic nature due to a complex interaction of broader technology and internal funding cycles. Mature projects in this study had gone through multiple generations of development. To fully understand them, it was necessary to gather extensive information about the project beyond the current iteration. It was sometimes even difficult to establish clear boundaries between projects. Finally, some projects were designed to achieve transient goals rather than long-term continuation, so the question of success for these projects was more one of impact than survival. The best way to determine their success was through establishing the influence and connections they had to other projects.

A significant body of aggregated information about educational computing projects is critical for tracking the evolution of individual projects and the relationships among them over multiple generations. Aggregating information can start with sets of data like that obtained from catalogs, summaries or reports. Then it is essential to use a weighting scheme to determine when to pursue targeted documentation such as published findings. Finally, it is critical to include detailed accounts from interviews and internal documents obtained through case studies. Unfortunately, the level and amount of data that can be collected by individual researchers varies directly with their level of access to projects. This presents a dilemma for large-scale investigations of the history of educational computing. Luckily, the most detailed data and accurate insights are best obtained from those who worked on the project, so a productive approach is to create ways for the participants themselves to contribute information.

These points have led the original research project reported above to gradually evolve towards emphasizing negotiation and cooperation to obtain and include data from the participants in educational computing projects, working simultaneously bottom up and top down. The project is thus transforming into a collaborative community resource where project participants can share knowledge. This approach will support an expedition to understand the complex relationships among key factors in the educational, technical and organizational contexts within and between educational computing projects across a variety of disciplines and levels as they change over time. A key component of this approach will also be to advocate ongoing longitudinal data collection and preservation within the projects themselves, and then to document where the project information resides and what it contains so others might use it.

Ever since the original study, computing technology was used to support data collection, analysis and reporting, but the new direction presents a technical challenge that will require a powerful digital environment for storing and integrating information. This parallels developments in a related field. Scholars who study the recent history of science and technology have undertaken digital projects focused on automation and collaboration with living participants. One of the most recognized among these initiatives is the History of Recent Science and Technology (HRST) funded by the Sloan Foundation and centered at the Dibner Institute at the Massachusetts Institute of Technology.

> A great hope of the HRST founders was that this website would be used primarily by scientists and engineers, experts in their own fields, who would select most important primary sources and deposit them on the site, compile timelines and bibliographies, add comments, and organize online discussions. Historians working on the project would largely serve as facilitators, helping the primary users to cope with the intricacies of the Web technology. The website itself would serve as the true engine of historical research. (Gerovitch, 2002)

In the future, the original research project that has been the subject of this paper will evolve into an appropriate technical environment to support follow-up and further elaboration about the projects already studied (Mitchell & Dertouzos, 1997). Projects that are closely related to those already studied will be added. This might include PLATO from the University of Illinois (Alpert & Bitzer, 1970) as well as cT and Andrew at Carnegie Mellon University (Arms, 1988, 1990). Most importantly, an investigation of the development of the computer language Logo will serve as the primary pilot for the next phase of this research (Papert, 1980). It is an excellent project to investigate due to it's robust and ongoing success, it's durability over many generations of computing paradigms, it's focus on a wide range of audiences from children to adult, and most importantly, it's great success in the international arena. Data about how and why it has succeeded around the globe will be sought from people associated with the Logo community on every continent.

5. CONCLUSION

This paper has described how a project to study the factors that influence success in educational computing projects evolved from historical case studies carried out in the early 1990s to the point of transition where it is today. While the long-term goal of the project continues to be improving the viability of educational computing projects by identifying and disseminating effective and sustainable strategies, how to go about it has evolved greatly. Specific limitations encountered in the original study's methodology drove the project to transform into using negotiation and cooperation for collecting and comparing broader and more in-depth historical data. This process may be a first step towards understanding where the field of educational computing has been, how successful it has been and why. Ultimately, this project could serve as a disciplinary memory for the uses of computers in education. Having such a memory broadly available for analysis could potentially make it easier to determine ways to go forward with both existing and new projects more successfully in the future.

REFERENCES

Alpert, D. and Bitzer, D., 1970, Advances in computer-based education. *Science* **167**: 1582-1590

Arfman, J.M. and Roden, P., 1992, Project Athena: Supporting distributed computing, *IBM Systems Journal* **31**(3): 550-563.

Arms, W. Y., 1988, *Andrew Plus: Personal Computing at Carnegie Mellon*, Carnegie Mellon University, Pittsburgh, PA.

Arms, W. Y., 1990, Reflections on Andrew, *EDUCOM Review*, **25**(3): 33-39.

Beeman, W. O., Anderson, K. T., Bader, G., Larkin, J., McClard, A. P., McQuillan, P. and Shields, M., 1987, *Intermedia: A Case Study of Innovation in Higher Education. Providence*, Brown University Office of Program Analysis, Institute for Research in Information and Scholarship, Providence, RI

Borg, W. R. and Gall, M. D., et al., 1989, *Educational Research: An Introduction*, 5th ed., Longman Publishing, New York, NY.

Bucciarelli, L., 1992, *Results of Survey of Student use of Athena-Based Problem Solutions*, unpublished raw data, MIT, Cambridge, MA.

Bucciarelli, L. and LaVin, A. R., 1992, 2.01: The mechanics of solids, and Athena: A conversation with Larry Bucciarelli, *Athena Insider: The Academic Computing Services Newsletter*, **3** (1): 6-11.

Champine, G. A., 1991, *MIT Project Athena: A Model for Distributed Campus Computing*, Digital Press, Cambridge, MA.

Einstein, H., 1991, Engineering Geology Educator, in C. Avril, ed., *Windows on Athena: Vol. 2: Project Athena's Curriculum Development Projects...And Beyond*, MIT, Cambridge, MA.

Gerovitch, S., 2002, *Toward an Interactive History of Science and Technology: Reflections on the Dibner/Sloan Web Project*, paper presented at the LXV plenum of the Russian National Committee of the History and Philosophy of Science and Technology, Moscow.

Hopper, M. E., LeBold, W. K., and Feghali, A. A., 1991, A hypermedia-based problem-solving approach to engineering, learning, working, and playing, in *Proceedings of the 1991 Frontiers in Education Conference*, pp. 73-78.

Hopper, M.E., 1997, *The Role of Learners in the Construction of Successful Courseware Projects in Distributed Academic Computing Environments*, round-table presentation at the Annual Meeting of American Educational Research Association, Advanced Technologies for Learning (SIG-ATL), Chicago, IL.

Hopper, M. E., 1994, Usable software in advanced educational computing projects, *ACM SIGGRAPH Computer Graphics*, 28(1): 46-48.

Hopper, M.E., 1993, Expert's views about key issues for courseware development in advanced computing environments [Abstract], in H. Maurer, ed., *Proceedings of ED-MEDIA 93 - World Conference on Educational Multimedia and Hypermedia*, p. 607.

Hopper, M. E., 1993, *Educational Courseware Production in Advanced Computing Environments*, unpublished doctoral dissertation, Purdue University, West Lafayette, IN.

Jackson, G., 1991, Conclusion: Project Athena in the evolution of academic computing at MIT, in C. Avril, ed., *Windows on Athena: Vol.2: Project Athena's Curriculum Development Projects...And Beyond*, MIT, Cambridge, MA.

Kinnicutt, P., 1992, *Engineering Geology Tutor 1.32/1.38 Questionnaire General Comments*, unpublished data, MIT Department of Civil Engineering, Cambridge, MA.

Launhardt, J. and Kahn, P., 1991, *The Educational Uses of Intermedia* (Tech. Rep. No 91-2), Brown University Institute for Research in Information and Scholarship, Providence, RI.

Landow, G. P., 1989, Course assignments using hypertext: The example of Intermedia, *Journal of Research on Computing in Education*, **21**: 349-365.

LeBold, W. K., Hopper, M. E., and Feghali, A. A., 1991, A hypermedia solution to a hyper problem: Personalized computer engineering career system, in *Proceedings of the 1991 ASEE-IEEE Annual Conference* (Educational Research and Methods Division), pp. 482-488.

Lerman, S., 1987, *Mission and Goals for Project Athena After June 1988*, MIT Project Athena, Cambridge, MA.

Marshall, C. and Rossman, G. B., 1989, *Designing Qualitative Research*, Sage Publications, Newbury Park, CA.

McClintock, R., 1986, Into the starting gate: On computing and the curriculum, *Teacher's College Record*, 88(2).

McCune, J. E., 1989, The TODOR workshop: Computer-enhanced teaching of fluid mechanics, in C. Avril, ed., *Windows on Athena: Project Athena's Curriculum Development Projects*, Project Athena, Cambridge, MA.

Meyrowitz, N., 1986, Intermedia: The architecture and construction of an object-oriented hypertext/hypermedia system and applications framework, *ACM SIGPLAN Notices* **21**(11): 186-201.

Meyrowitz, N., 1991, Hypertext - does it reduce cholesterol, too? in Nyce, J. and Kahn, P. eds., *From Memex to Hypertext: Vanevar Bush and the Mind's Machine*, Academic Press, pp. 287-318.

MIT Committee on Academic Computation for the 1990's and Beyond, 1990, *Computing for Education at MIT: Final Report*, MIT, Cambridge, MA.

Mitchell, W. J. and Dertouzos, M. L., 1997, *MIT Educational Technology Council Report*, MIT, Cambridge, MA.

Molnar, A., 1990, Computers in education: A historical perspective of the unfinished task, *THE Journal* **18**(4): 80-83.

Murman, E. M., 1987, *Computer Enhanced Curriculum For Fluid Mechanics: A Progress Report*, MIT, Cambridge, MA.

Murman, E. M., LaVin, A. R. and Ellis, S. C., 1988, *Enhancing Fluid Mechanics Education with Workstation Based Software,* AIAA Paper 88-0001 Paper presented at the AIAA 26th Aerospace Sciences Meeting January 11-14, 1988, Reno, Nevada.

Office of Technology Assessment, 1988, *Power on!: New Tools for Teaching and Learning*, Congress of the U. S., Office of Technology, Washington, DC.

Papert, S., 1980, *Mindstorms: Children, Computers, and Powerful Ideas*, Basic Books, NY.

Stewart, J., 1989, How to manage educational computing initiatives-lessons from the first five years of Project Athena at MIT, in E. Barrett, ed., *The Society of Text: Hypertext, Hypermedia and the Social Construction of Information*, MIT Press, Cambridge MA, pp. 284-321.

Taylor, R. P. (Ed.), 1980, *The Computer in the School: Tutor, Tool, Tutee*, Teachers College Press, New York, NY.

Trilling, L., 1988, *AERO/ASTRO Students' Reaction to the Use of Athena Materials in Fluid Mechanics*, MIT Department of Aeronautics and Astronautics, Cambridge, MA.

Yankelovich, N., Meyrowitz, N. and VanDam, A., 1985, Reading and writing the electronic book, *IEEE Computer*, **18**(10): 15-30.

USING COMPUTING HISTORY TO ENHANCE TEACHING

John Impagliazzo and John A.N. Lee
Hofstra University, USA; Virginia Tech and Radford University, USA
E-mail: cscjzi@Hofstra.edu; janlee17@verizon.net

Abstract: This paper focuses on a "history approach" as a way of teaching courses in computing. This project, funded in part by the National Science Foundation of the United States, is to use history as an ongoing theme throughout a course through the adaptation of relevant historical materials. The paper shows how the authors used historical materials to enhance course delivery. The expectation is that using history can make for a positive change in a course from one of sterile factual content to one containing dynamic interludes involving people, places, and events. In this manner, computing courses should be much more interesting. This mode of teaching should also stimulate more students (non-specialists) to consider computing as their major field of study.

Key words: History; Education; Case studies; Pedagogical tools

1. INTRODUCTION

Using history as a pedagogical tool should contribute to students' life-long learning experiences, encourage students from diverse and minority communities to appreciate computing, and increase student retention. Students should also gain a better sense of the nature of inquiry, the processes of innovation, and the human dimension.

In the beginning one of the major drawbacks to developing courses in the history of computing in educational institutions was the lack of reliable resources, trained teachers, and institutional support. While we believe that the case for using history in the normal compliment of courses, institutional support has been sadly lacking. History is not commonly a subject that leads to industrial development or has significant advantages in maintaining a business presence in the marketplace. History is not a subject that attracts significant research grants (as compared to other grants in the IT field) and is not of great advantage to a faculty member when being considered for promotion or tenure. To a lesser extent computing education suffers from similar drawbacks as a topic of concentration in research universities.

Within a computing curriculum, the inclusion of a study of historical elements has the advantages that it will require computing students to "think outside the box" for a while, and particularly, outside the box defined by the computer perched before them. Assuming that a study module is more than a lecture style presentation and that students will "research" the topic themselves, history will force computing students to look beyond the machine and language manuals, and thereby broaden their outlook on the world. History modules must be more than just the recitation of anecdotes, though this may be a good place to tweak their interest. Using history as a subject of study has the advantage of requiring students to do some library research beyond the world wide web, to write more than comments in program headers, and perform some critical thinking that is not necessarily algorithmic—all subjects that are not the favorites of computing majors, but which need reinforcement. A subject such as computer science is not famous for its case studies as an educational methodology, but history may be able to provide the resources to foster this approach to computing education.

Why use history? While the tenet of this paper is the ability to enhance greatly the teaching of computing by using history as a medium, many other benefits exist that we cannot ignore. Among these are the concerns that unless we understand the history of the field, then we may be doomed to repeat the past. In many instances, the study of history can resurrect ideas and concepts that either progress overcame or were ahead of their time. For example, students who have grown up in the UNIX environment may be familiar with `lex` and `yacc` as means of language analysis, but when faced with another environment, they are unable to apply the more fundamental concepts of finite state machines to a similar problem. Though the center of computing is the inanimate objects of hardware and software, computing was the invention of pioneers whom we should neither forget nor deny their due credit.

History can also promote curiosity that overcomes the beliefs of many that "history is past" and has no modern value, or that science progresses to overcome its past. Unfortunately, in the eyes of professional historians computer history is too recent to be history and too recent to be forgotten. Chronological history is easy to present and readily available in many places, but like the history we were taught in high school it is without meaning unless it is related to other fields of study. History is mostly the history of successes since the "winners" write most of history. Yet we could learn much from our failures.

Using history as an educational tool is giving students the ability to know how to build on the past and to follow Isaac Newton's testimonial that "If I have seen a little further than others, it is because I have stood on the shoulders of giants."

2. HISTORY IN THE COMPUTING CURRICULUM

It is appropriate that one make a clear distinction between a course in the history of a subject and incorporating history into the curriculum, and between teaching history as part of the curriculum and requiring students to take a course in history. A 1998 IFIP report produced by a joint committee selected from TC-3 and WG9.7 provided the resources for the construction of several different styles of history course in computing (Impagliazzo et al, 1998).

The report justifies the establishment of a history component in the computing curriculum by providing a framework for a curriculum and its supporting resources. It was international in scope and is not confined it specific computing disciplines. It also sought to raise the awareness of history and the manner in which people could use it to improve the study and practice of the computing profession. The report recommended guidelines on how history could be included as a part of computer education at the college or university level. The report suggested three ways of carrying this out:

- An integrated approach where history becomes a part of existing courses;
- A single course for computing specialists who have completed at least one year of study in their specialty; or
- A single course with no prerequisite open to all students.

These modes varied in the depth of presentation and the courses offered in the respective programs. The approach taken by this report was to propose a knowledge base of suggested historical topics, including current events. Irrespective of the mode of implementation, the topics contained in the knowledge base suggest a possible course framework. Teachers can customize the knowledge base according to the needs of their individual programs. For the integrated approach, teachers can incorporate the historical topics into existing courses. It is this latter approach that we consider further herein.

3. HISTORY IN THE FIRST COURSE

In any curriculum, the introductory course is the key to maintaining students' interest and enthusiasm, and encouraging them to persevere to comprehend the concepts and fundamentals, and where appropriate to develop skills that will serve them well in the rest of the curriculum. Computer Science has had two "traditional" introductory courses – a "computer literacy" course and a beginning programming course. In terms of "Curriculum 1991" [Tucker et al, 1991] these are generally designated as courses CS0 and CS1. While some may assume that the content of the literacy course is part of the high school preparatory repertoire in many curricula, such content is an essential element of a program of study, laying the groundwork for many later courses. It also demonstrates to the participants that there is more to the field of computing than just programming, and more to computing than what one can do on a modern computer.

The approach taken by these authors was to develop a learning plan that is primarily a "grand tour" of computer science that can easily be tailored to the curriculum of most any particular program. Like a geographical grand tour, the introduction to computer science should explore the main avenues of the subject, with enough of a view of the alleys and byways to suggest to the traveler that they can come back later and explore on their own, or pick up another tour guide (in another course) to look at the deeper details. A tour-bus in a major city shows tourists where they might find primary sites; similarly, introductory courses show the locations and facades of the key topics within computing areas.

Abstract machines are easy to ascribe to their originators and this is one more opportunity to teach something of our history. For example, the study of compilers as a tool of computer scientists includes the study of finite state machines for lexical analysis. The study will also show that simple syntactic analyzers relate to context-free languages as specified in Backus-Normal Form (BNF), sometimes also known as Backus-Naur Form. The contribution of McCulloch and Pitts, in developing the ideas of finite state machines as a model of nervous behavior in the brain is an example of how we have assembled the foundations of computer science from a variety of sources [McCulloch and Pitts, 1943] and conversely the applicability of computer technology to other fields. The history of programming languages starting from the early determination of develop "automatic programming" (a goal still not achieved) through the concept of the compiler and eventually to the demonstration of the practicality of high level programming languages through FORTRAN and COBOL is an important lesson for beginning students [Wexelblat, 1981, and Bergin and Gibson, 1996].

Following up on the claim that Alan Turing was one of the five original inventors of the computer is a study of the "universal machine" that he prescribed in his 1937 paper on computable numbers [Turing, 1937]. While there possibly exist some emulators of the early machines, the opportunity to program an original computer, limited as it is, is of great interest to our modern students. The opportunity to examine this machine and to show that Turing's claim to universality is important to the understanding of the foundations of the field, even if this initial exploration is minimal. However, the study of abstract machines is a meaningful event in the "grand tour" with the understanding that a later course will follow up on these basics. Study of the Turing Machine provides the occasion to discuss the life story of Alan Turing [Hodges, 1983] and his many other contributions to the field of computing and to other fields such as biology. Not the least of his work was the code breaking at Bletchley Park during World War II. This is one case also where there is available a one-hour NOVA video program entitled *The Strange Life and Times of Alan Turing*, which can provide details beyond the capabilities of most teachers. A course on the fundamentals of computers and computing is by its very nature a course on the history of computing.

4. HISTORY AS A SOURCE FOR CASE STUDIES

With a basis of using history in the first course as a "humanizing" element in the teaching of technology, it is appropriate to be able to follow up on this in subsequent courses. After all, the introductory course is simply the "grand tour" and thus students will expect to find details in the ensuing courses. This presumes that besides the teachers of the introductory course, faculty members in other courses are familiar with the history of the field. This raises the question regarding the requisiteness of teachers of technology being conversant with the history of at least the technology they teach. For several decades, computer science has ignored its history in favor of a forwarding-looking approach that ignores the postulate that those who ignore history are doomed to repeat it. While the professional organizations, primarily the Association for Computing Machinery (ACM) and the IEEE Computer Society, have contributed to the preservation of our history in many ways, the coverage of the field is still "spotty". ACM organized several conferences in the fifteen years after 1978 entitled "The History of ...", the most famous of which were the History of Programming Languages conferences in 1978 and 1993, there is still need to look back at the histories of (say) operating systems, human computer interaction, or specific subjects such as object oriented programming. Moreover, most specialized textbooks do not contain a section on the history of the subject, and unfortunately, where it is included it contains many of the myths discussed above simply because the authors do not have ready access to original materials or documents.

One solution to this problem is for the computer historians in departments of computer science to organize a "while you are away" program as teacher substitutes with the understanding that they will give a lesson on the history of computing relative to the course topic. By videotaping the presentation, providing a set of slides/overhead foils, or a PowerPoint presentation, this component can become a permanent part of the course. Working with the instructor can also identify the points on the curve of perceived complexity of development from which teachers can extract learning points to create a better course plan using history to teach the topic [Lee, 2000].

We can see the "proof" of the concept by considering the perceived complexity of a number of developments in our field. For example, the development of operating systems for personal computers from CP/M through MS Windows is an excellent case study that shows how attitudes changed over the years. CP/M, though extremely simple in concept was viewed as the domain of the microprocessor priesthood and thus extremely complex to the general user. DOS for the IBM-PC improved this perception, but the original operating system for the Apple Macintosh marks the point where the general user was accepting of the notion of a helpful operating system. Since that time, enhancements and "improvements" have generated a Windows operating system that some people regard as "complex" even though many use it. The "understandability" of operating systems for PCs improved from the time of the CP/M system to the Mac OS, but decreased thereafter. Similar trends appear in programming languages from FORTRAN to Ada, with a second overlapping curve showing the perceived complexity changes from the original C language to Java. Such secondary curves clearly indicate that someone decided to step outside the box and to solve the problem of perceived complexity.

5. HISTORY IN A PROFESSIONALISM COURSE

History can also be a source of case studies for use in courses related to ethics and social impact. While a community interested in computer ethics has developed a large number of scenarios for use in their courses, the reality of a truly historical case provides link to the world that is not found in synthesized examples. Examples include studying the questions:

- Did John Mauchly really base the arithmetic unit of the ENIAC on the ABC?

- What was the impact of the 1956 IBM consent decree on business practices in the computing field?
- Could people have avoided the Therac 25 problems?
- Should computer pioneers have been more protective of their inventions?

The collection of cases is another of those under-developed aspect of the history of computing. This is primarily the result of our being overly protective of the sensitivity of developers whose projects were not successful. Our archival journals rarely contain technical articles on why an article failed or did not succeed, and locating the original documentation, if any, is nigh on impossible. The archives of the Charles Babbage Institute at the University of Minnesota are one potential source of cases, but so far, their funding for detailed examination of the deposited materials has been minimal. Surely, the material is there! However, we cannot expect teachers to go looking for it; that is the task of historians. We truly need to share our resources so that others can benefit from these positive experiences.

6. HISTORY IN THE COMPUTER ARCHITECTURE COURSE

The computer architecture course, a common part of most curricula in computer science, is typical of those in which attention to history is most important and revealing. It would be inappropriate to introduce students to computers without discussing the "invention" of the computer and discussing the question of who had the inspiration. Even a discussion of what constitutes a computer and how a computer is different from a calculator is essential. Here is an opportunity also for providing students with an overview of the meaning of the word computer, and to understand that in the days before the word computer was ascribed to a physical device it was first ascribed to people who ran calculators for scientists and engineers. While firsts are always difficult to identify, an opportunity exists within this course to give proper credit to national pioneers who were the first in the country of the students to either build or install a computer. Hardware is often the focus of computing history since it is easy to recognize, but contributions to theory and software also significant.

How many typical computing students have ever held, touched, or even seen a computer or its components? Since computer science or any of its related fields center on the software and applications aspects, few students hardly ever receive exposure to the electrical and electronic elements of a computer. Few have ever held resistors or capacitors, transistors, vacuum tubes, memory chips, floppy disks, or motherboards. Looking at the generations of computer development is an opportunity to examine these artifacts and to begin to understand the space and heat problems of early machines. Disassembling components also helps in understanding.

Today's machines have a "customary" memory hierarchy devised in the early days. While it seems natural today, the history of the development of hierarchical memories as proposed in 1962 by Tom Kilburn and demonstrated with the Atlas at Manchester University brings out the priority of invention in the years before IBM System/360. Similarly, the development of the cache, proposed by Maurice Wilkes in 1965 in short paper, and first implemented at Cambridge University preceded the first commercial machine to use cache – the IBM 360/85. From these ideas came virtual memory, an idea that is inherent in most modern day machines.

The story of pipeline methodologies and dynamic scheduling, introduced in the CDC 6600 in 1964, "the First supercomputer" leads to explanations of multiple function units, score-boarding, time-shared pipeline, and the Tomasulo algorithm. From there it is a short step to RISC machines and the contributions of John Cocke, in the mid-1980s, that led to IBM Power 1 and Power machine series.

Behind the potentially sterile views of hardware and computer architecture are stories. We can use these stories to help students understand the progress of development and to understand better how things have come together as a conglomeration of elements. Ultimately, we can show how these events have coalesced into the machines of today.

7. STORIES AND INTRODUCTORY COURSES

So, how do we involve history in our courses? How can historical story telling make computing courses more interesting? Our focus here relates to introductory courses. These courses often take an "overview" approach and students attending them come from a variety of specialties. Introductory courses often have a heterogeneous mix of students requiring the instructor to take inventive measures to retain student attention. Using computing history is one way to do this.

One program that attempts to change the way students learn in computing courses is a project at Hofstra University where history is a theme used within an existing introductory course. The course, called "Overview of Computer Science", educates over two thousand students each year. Students learn the breadth of computer science and receive some exposure to a simple programming language such as JavaScript. The project, called Computing History Resource Adaptation (CHRAD), receives partial funding through the National Science Foundation of the United States. In selected sections of this course, several teachers use history as a theme of presentation. For these course sections, students view two to three videos on the evolution of early computers, the history of software, and one on women and computing. Students also receive written summaries of these videos for reference. Students also explore computing history through various collections at virtual museums such as the Computer History Museum in California, the Charles Babbage Institute in Minnesota, the IEEE History Center, the American Computer Museum in Montana, and other museums worldwide.

The project has also developed other historical tools to facilitate a student's ability to research computing history. These include historical timelines and chronologies, and historical "slices" according to the knowledge areas found in the Computing Curricula 2001. In addition, the project developed other focused areas related to computing history such as the antitrust cases with Microsoft, the evolution of the transistor, and DNA and quantum computing. The project describes the latter two areas in an elementary manner rather than in a rigorous way to accommodate the abilities of the intended students.

The result of the CHRAD project is very positive. When compared to sections that do not use the history approach, students were able to identify computing pioneers and had a "human" insight into the computing world. Attendance levels for the history sections were almost perfect. All students, save a very few, completed the course and almost no student had failed. Students appeared engaged and interested in computing and because of the history theme, could relate computing to people and places with a temporal perspective. Computing did not appear to them as a dry subject of concepts and abstractions. Rather, computing became alive where the dynamics of life interwove with the subject content. Students seemed to connect and with the subject material and the course developed into a true liberal arts subject. For most students in this introductory course, the history approach has mitigated the "fear" of taking a computer course and has made them "connect" with the subject in a human way.

From a personal viewpoint, teaching computing from a historical perspective was and is simply fun. Bridging story telling with technical content forms a connection between the subject and the student that seems to form a true basis for lifelong learning. All teachers should try this approach with their computing classes!

8. SUMMARY

It is probably unlikely that commercial publishers will provide textbooks in the field that cover specialized studies of computer history in individual subjects. However, we should be encouraging authors of technical textbooks to include a section the background history, authored in cooperation with a historian. Similarly, we need to encourage online virtual museums to go beyond being collections of images to providing "walk-through" galleries of that will provide deeper descriptions of specialized histories. In fact, museums should merely be portals to distributed digital libraries to resources with intelligent assimilation systems to permit teachers and students to construct custom-selected study guides. One such resource could be constructed from the volumes of the *Annals of the History of Computing*, that already contains (now in a digitized form through the IEEE Computer Society digital library) many of the stories of computing distributed across formal articles, memoirs, anecdotes, and obituaries.

Clearly, there is a need to persuade granting agencies and foundations to support the development of these resources. Reluctance exists to fund extensive projects in the history of computing on the excuse that the principals are not "trained historians", in a time when the number of so-qualified individuals is extremely small. Just as many early computer scientists themselves were not educated within the computer science discipline so computer historians are primarily "self-grown". Computer scientists with advice from historians of technology must lead the impetus for recording and recovering the history of computing to create the encyclopedia of the history of computing to support computer education.

REFERENCES

ACM / IEEE Computer Society, "Computing Curriculum 2001", (Final Report http://www.computer.org/education/cc2001/final/index.htm),

Bergin, Thomas J. and Richard G. Gibson, 1996, *The History of Programming Languages - II*, Addison-Wesley Pub. Co., 864 pp.

Godfrey, M.D., and D.F. Hendry, 1993, "The Computer as von Neumann Planned It", *IEEE Annals of the History of Computing*, Vol. 15, No. 1, pp. 11-21.

Hodges, Andrew, 1983, *Alan Turing: The Enigma*, Simon and Shuster, New York.

Impagliazzo John, et al., 1998, History in the Computing Curriculum. IFIP TC 3 / TC 9 Joint Task Group, http://www.hofstra.edu/pdf/CompHist_9810rprt.PDF (See also: *IEEE Annals of the History of Computing*, Vol 21, No 1, pp. 1-15, January 1999.)

Lee, J.A.N., 2000, "Perceived Complexity: A Conjecture Regarding the Life Cycle of Computer-Related Products", IFIP World Computer Congress 2000, Beijing China, August 2000.

McCulloch, Warren S., and Walter Pitts, 1943, "A Logical Calculus of the Ideas Immanent in Nervous Activity", *Bull. Math. Biophysics*, Vol. 5, pp. 115-133.

Tucker, Allen B., et al., 1991, Computing Curricula '91. Association for Computing Machinery and the Computer Society of the Institute of Electrical and Electronics Engineers.

Turing, Alan M., 1937, "On Computable Numbers with an Application to the Entscheidungsproblem", *Proc. London Math. Soc.*, Vol. 42, pp. 230-65.[6]

Wexelblat, Richard L., 1981, *The History of Programming Languages*, Academic Press, 758 pp.

Williams, Michael R., 1997, *A History of Computing Technology*, Second Edition, IEEE Computer Society Press, March 1997, 440 pp.

Zemanek, Heinz, 1979, "Al-Khorezmi: His Background, His Personality, His Work, and His Influence", *Symp. Algorithms in Modern Mathematics and Computer Science*, Urgench, Uzbek, USSR, September 1979.

ENDNOTE

The National Science Foundation of the United States supported part of this work.

[6] This paper defined the concept of the Universal Machine.

Appendix

Due to circumstances beyond his control, Meir Komar could not complete his paper in time for publication. We include here an abstract. The paper appears at the URL <http://sukka.jct.ac.il/~komar/HCE2004>. The title, abstract, and keywords appear below.

-- John Impagliazzo and JAN Lee, Co-Editors

THE EVOLUTION OF THE CS TEACHER IN ISRAEL – THE FIRST GENERATION

Meir Komar
Jerusalem College of Technology, Israel
E-mail: komar@jct.ac.il

Abstract: Computer Science (CS) was introduced, as an elective into the Israeli matriculation program in 1974. The introduction of an entirely new discipline required the creation of an appropriate inspectorate within the framework of the Ministry of Education. In addition to defining the curriculum, the inspectorate had to initiate the training and accreditation process for a CS teacher. The emerging CS teacher was confronted by many varied issues. For example, the lack of textbooks, rapidly changing technologies and school administrations' ignorance of computers in general and specifically what is computer science. This paper shows how these key issues were addressed and the methodologies that were implemented to train the "first generation" of CS teachers in Israel.

Keywords: Secondary level, Israel, Teachers

APPLICATION OF SOFTWARE AGENTS IN INFORMATION RETRIEVAL IN VIRTUAL LEARNING SYSTEM IN BULGARIA

Poster Abstract

Teodora Ivanova Bakardjieva and Boyka Gradinarova
Varna Free University, Bulgaria; Varna Technical University, Bulgaria
E-mail: bakardjieva@vfu.bg; inflot@mbox.digsys.bg

Abstract: Nowadays, the internet technologies and software agents are becoming increasingly important in online learning systems. Web-based training and the use of agents offer the opportunities to enhance traditional courses, encourage life-long learning and enable more people to join the learning society. Software agents prove to be the necessary tool in improving the effectiveness and efficiency of retrieval in such systems.

The paper presents main concepts about software agents and discusses their advantages in optimizing the retrieval process. This study explores the application of software agents in information retrieval processes in web-based applications for online learning systems. The outlined objectives are to develop a methodology for agent learning of user preferences in every user session and to integrate an information retrieval algorithm. The agent will make its own base on the user's preferences. The research is made at Varna Free University and an interactive learning system new for Bulgaria, is proposed..

Keywords: University Level, WCCE, Software Development, Learning Management Systems, Projects

MIX
Papier aus verantwortungsvollen Quellen
Paper from responsible sources
FSC® C105338

If you have any concerns about our products,
you can contact us on
ProductSafety@springernature.com

In case Publisher is established outside the EU,
the EU authorized representative is:
Springer Nature Customer Service Center GmbH
Europaplatz 3, 69115 Heidelberg, Germany

Printed by Libri Plureos GmbH
in Hamburg, Germany